JOB OFFER!

A HOW-TO NEGOTIATION GUIDE

Maryanne L.
Wegerbauer

jist
Publishing

S

JOB OFFER!: A How-To Negotiation Guide

© 2000 by Maryanne L. Wegerbauer

Published by JIST Works, Inc.
8902 Otis Avenue
Indianapolis, IN 46216
1-800-648-5478
E-Mail: jistworks@aol.com

Visit our Web site for information on other JIST products:
http://www.jist.com

Editor: Lori Cates
Copy Editor: Erik Dafforn
Proofreader: Becca York
Interior and Cover Design: designLab, Seattle

Printed in the United States of America.

Cataloging-in-Publication Data is on file with the Library of Congress.

03 02 01 00   9 8 7 6 5 4 3 2 1

We have been careful to provide accurate information throughout this book, but it is possible that errors and omissions have been introduced. Please consider this in making any important decisions. Trust your own judgment above all else and in all things.

We are grateful to the American Compensation Association for permission to reproduce the definitions contained in the "Glossary of Compensation and Benefits Terms" at the end of this book.

ISBN: 1-56370-666-0

Dedication

For Mike and Jim, who are always there for me when the cards are down.

About the Author

Maryanne L. Wegerbauer has personal and professional experience "from both sides of the table" with the concepts contained in *Job Offer!* Her career in human resource management began in 1984, when Maryanne joined the human resources department of a Fortune 500 company in Hartford, Connecticut. Due to ongoing reorganization and re-engineering throughout her tenure there, Maryanne had the opportunity to work in a capacity that not only drew on her compensation and benefits expertise, but also necessitated broad generalist knowledge. Her work called for an understanding of staffing and employee issues and demonstrated consulting, counseling, and individual and group communication skills. It implicitly required a strong understanding of the principles and concepts of organizational change.

As a member of the American Compensation Association, The Society for Human Resource Management, and the Professional Placement Network, Maryanne has been active for many years in professional associations. She has led and worked on committees and made presentations at numerous human resource seminars, conferences, and industry survey group meetings.

A longtime Connecticut resident who recently relocated to Florida, Maryanne's perspective in *Job Offer!* is grounded in her own positive experience with flexible working arrangements. She actively engaged in volunteer and flextime work while bringing up her children.

Maryanne has a bachelor's degree from The University of Connecticut and also holds Certified Compensation Professional (CCP) and Certified Benefits Professional (CBP) designations. She is the author of a student guide, *Report Writing: Formula for Success* (The Continental Press, Inc.).

Contents

Introduction

ABOUT THIS GUIDE

In these changing times, with employers competing for skilled workers, the individual wields increased negotiating power. Now more than ever, job candidates must know what options are available and understand how to negotiate their terms of employment. Likewise, managers and recruiters must recognize what job-offer variables are within their control so that they can construct a package aimed at attracting *and retaining* employees with indispensable, in-demand job skills.

This book guides both the hiring manager and the successful job applicant through the final, critical preemployment step: the process of negotiating the conditions of the job offer.

Today, the growing segment of small and midsize companies is hiring more people. The owners and managers of these companies, while open to innovation, may not be fully knowledgeable about flexible benefits and creative work-reward arrangements. The purpose of this book is to stimulate communication between employers and potential and current employees by exploring the many facets of the employment package. The information will assist in framing attractive and competitive job and compensation covenants and facilitate the construction of mutually rewarding agreements.

On the premise that almost anything and everything is negotiable, the best way to approach a job offer or opportunity is to be thoroughly familiar with the many elements—tangible and intangible—that will combine to make up a candidate's future work environment. This book provides an across-the-board examination of compensation and benefits program components. It discusses the variables of job design and content, and it sets the stage for negotiation by observing the nature of organizations. It describes the negotiation process and enables the reader to apply the principles of negotiation to job offers.

Job Offer! includes tips, planning checklists, and worksheets for ranking and comparing offer arrangements. It also includes a comprehensive compensation and benefits glossary for reference as you determine and prioritize work-reward parameters.

WHO CAN BENEFIT FROM THIS BOOK?

The insights in this book are helpful for people on both sides of the negotiation table. And even if you already have a job, you can use this book to help negotiate a better situation.

JOB SEEKERS

This book begins at the point at which a job has been offered. You must decide whether to accept it and under what terms. Discussion focuses on constructing the best possible employment package.

Although salary is often considered the focus of job offers and negotiations, a number of other components collectively make up the total offer package, such as insurance, bonuses, days off, and special work arrangements—for example, flextime and telecommuting. This book contains extensive information about various offer elements and includes worksheets to help you determine which options are important enough to make or break a deal.

EMPLOYERS

Today it is expected that workers will change jobs—even careers—every five to seven years on average. Companies that offer a variety of packages have the advantage in recruiting qualified people. Cost-benefit analysis has shown that flexible arrangements, carefully managed, are of significant value in the workplace because they increase employee satisfaction and productivity. This book helps you discover how to secure the best possible mix of work-reward components for your recruits and, as a result, bring the talent you need on board and reduce turnover.

Job Offer! creates a basis for dialogue between employers and employees and a foundation for periodic job negotiations with valued employees you want to retain. It also serves as a management-planning resource for reviewing and refining compensation and benefits programs and creating realistic win-win conditions at work.

THE CURRENTLY EMPLOYED

This book is equally valuable for working out optimal arrangements for your current position. Combine the tips and advice in the book with your understanding of how your job has evolved, how you have managed your work, and how you've contributed to the organization's success. You can then use this information to negotiate an improved work situation.

HOW TO USE THIS BOOK

The information in this book is organized into chapters within five broad sections. Designed to facilitate ease of use, the format of each chapter follows a consistent outline:

Viewpoint	Links the chapter's topic to the negotiation outlook.
What Is (Topic) All About?	Introduces, discusses, and summarizes the chapter's subject matter.
How Does (Topic) Affect You?	Identifies possible impacts of the topic on the job seeker.
From the Employer's Side of the Table	Looks at the topic from the perspective of the recruiter or hiring manager and the employing organization.
Points to Remember	Summarizes the chapter's key points.
Tips and Worksheets	Provides in-depth topic tips and planning worksheets.

SHORTCUTS FOR SPECIAL SITUATIONS

If you have to prepare for negotiations quickly:

- ◆ Read chapters 10 through 12: "Compensation," "Primary Employee Benefits," and "Additional Employee Benefits."

- ◆ Read chapter 7, "Phase I: Preparation."

If you need to get right to the bottom line:

- ◆ Review the table of contents.

- ◆ Select and flip to the chapters of interest to you.

- ◆ Scan the "Viewpoint" and "Points to Remember" sections.

- ◆ Use the worksheets for notes and planning.

If you are currently employed and anticipating a future job offer or workplace negotiation, or if you simply want a solid grounding in the many aspects of work-related negotiables:

- ◆ Work through the chapters in detail, in any order of interest. This will help you understand the context for negotiations and the factors involved in honing negotiation skills, as well as the many variables in the work arena with potential for negotiation.

- ◆ Use your current or most recent work arrangements to complete the worksheets.

If you'd like the "big picture:"

- ◆ Read through the text progressively, focusing on the narrative discussion and "Points to Remember."

If you are an employer considering new programs or updates to existing policy to attract skilled workers and retain valued staff:

+ Read through chapters 1 through 8, noting how the topic may be meaningful to the worker and consequential to the organization (particularly helpful are the "From the Employer's Side of the Table" sections).

+ Evaluate the variables in chapters 9 through 12, developing cost-benefit analyses to assess the affordability and reasonability of each program component.

+ Have your proposals reviewed by accounting, legal, communications, and other relevant experts before instituting changes in policies or procedures.

PART I

Negotiation Concepts

This section introduces the topic of negotiation to potential employees, current employees, and hiring managers. It defines the concept of relative power and includes a worksheet to help each party determine their strengths for the negotiation.

CHAPTER 1

Negotiating the Job Offer

NEGOTIATION VIEWPOINT

Negotiation requires gathering information and resources, planning, communicating, and making decisions to reach a goal or objective. Approaching the process with an open mind and a positive attitude frees you from negative or confining preconceptions. As with many things in life, your expectations will communicate themselves and influence the outcome of the negotiations. How you think about and handle negotiating will greatly affect the result.

Congratulations! You made it through the interview process. Both you and the hiring manager agree that you are the right person for the job. Now, however, you must negotiate the terms of the job offer. Be prepared for this last, important step in the conclusion of a job search, which finalizes

- The design of the job and its functions

- The salary level and bonus opportunity

- The work location and work schedule

- The employment benefits and the perquisites (perks) of the job

In addition to prioritizing your needs in each of these areas, it is useful to assess the structure and content of the job offer from the other person's perspective. As you review the initial offer, gauge how negotiable each component may be. The employer might have little flexibility to tailor one company-prescribed core benefit, but a great deal of latitude to reconfigure another part of the package. Conversely, you might feel strongly about some aspects of the employment offer, but be willing to sacrifice in other areas.

WHAT IS NEGOTIATION ALL ABOUT?

Negotiation is formulating the terms of a transaction in such a way that each party receives the maximum benefit from the agreement. Negotiating is not a commonplace occurrence in our society, nor are its tough relatives—bargaining, bartering, and trading—the norm, although all are routine in other parts of the world. But people in our society do negotiate every day. In fact, every time two people agree on the value of an exchange, a negotiation of sorts has taken place. For example: A novice accepts and follows guidance in exchange for learning how to improve his or her performance; a teacher provides mentoring—sharing of knowledge and expertise—and guidance in exchange for the satisfaction of helping. Both find the arrangement fulfilling.

For those who enjoy challenging the status quo, almost every situation holds the possibility for negotiation. And almost everything is negotiable.

HOW DOES NEGOTIATION AFFECT YOU?

Long a characteristic of unionized employment environments, negotiated work agreements between individual nonunion workers and their employers are becoming more prevalent today due to the changing nature and complexity of the job market.

Initially, many people dislike negotiating. Some think that negotiation makes them appear to be tricky, manipulative, or confrontational. Certainly the potential for damaging a newly formed relationship cannot be ignored—hard bargaining often creates resentment and defensiveness. Win-lose negotiating can lead in turn to a win-lose situation for you: You get what you wanted, but you start your new job with the handicap of having caused ill will during the negotiations.

Skilled negotiation, as opposed to hard bargaining, more frequently results in a win-win agreement. Astute negotiators know what they want and need and what the other party wants and needs from the exchange. They assess their *relative power*—their own strengths and those created by the particular situation—and approach the negotiations accordingly. Successful negotiators remain fully attuned to what the other party is saying, verbally and nonverbally, and how the other party is reading and reacting to their messages throughout the agreement process. Negotiation requires skills that can be acquired—first learned, and then progressively improved through practice.

FROM THE EMPLOYER'S SIDE OF THE TABLE

Employers too can be uncomfortable about the idea of negotiating; however, competition for good employees is fierce. In order to attract and keep superior people, companies must be willing to take the unique needs of potential and current employees into consideration.

Most hiring managers don't have total freedom in tailoring a job offer to a worker's ideal. Some employers may feel that they have made a firm offer and have already worked hard to create an attractive work environment, with generous benefits to accommodate their employees. Employer constraints may include established company policy and existing programs, and vigilance regarding cost containment. Nevertheless, open-mindedly researching and managing a job-offer negotiation with a prospective worker or a valued employee is often the most productive approach.

While one component of the offer may be, for various supportable reasons, nonnegotiable, another may be quite flexible. High-cost programs already in place (such as total relocation assistance) may not be fully utilized and offer room for exchange.

On the other hand, making an exception for one employee may set a precedent and raise concerns about fairness to other employees.

POINTS TO REMEMBER

- Job offers can be negotiated.
- Components of an offer include job content, compensation and benefits, time and location arrangements, and job-related perks.
- As the job market has changed, opportunities for negotiation have increased.

- Skilled negotiation greatly heightens the chances for a mutually satisfactory outcome.

- Relative power is an important factor in negotiations.

- You can learn and develop negotiation skills.

CHAPTER 2

Relative Power

NEGOTIATION VIEWPOINT

Relative power is perhaps the most critical concept of negotiations for participants to master. Each party to the negotiation has a certain degree of strength—the ability to supply or fulfill the "needs and wants" of the other party. Knowing your strengths and resources, your ability to respond to the needs of the other party, and your competition enables you to more accurately assess your bargaining position in relation to that of the other person.

WHAT IS RELATIVE POWER ALL ABOUT?

Relative power is the degree of influence each party has on the outcome of a negotiation. It is essentially a function of supply, demand, and the components thereof. Relative power is directly related to the number and desirability of the other options available to each party.

Factors contributing to the relative power of both employer and employee in designing work agreements include the following:

Business Climate

- The state of the economy and the industry

- The overall unemployment rate and the general employment picture

- The demand for industry- and profession-specific knowledge and skills

Company

- Profitability
- The employing company's place in the business cycle

    Start-up

    Growing/new market

    Stable/profitable

    Underperforming/turnaround organization

Hiring Manager

- Urgency of the business's need to fill the position
- Decision-making authority
- Staffing budget

Individual

- Availability of other opportunities
- Technical expertise, unique knowledge/skill set
- Resources (financial depth, networks, and so on)
- Level of competition/availability of other candidates for the position
- Career risk

HOW DOES RELATIVE POWER AFFECT YOU?

Reviewing the strengths that you bring to an employment situation helps you establish priorities as you prepare to negotiate the job offer.

Skilled and knowledgeable individuals have employment choices that allow them to positively influence the conditions of their employment. By remaining up-to-date in your professional area of expertise and keeping abreast of the employment market for specific skills, you can fairly assess what you are "bringing to the table." In some instances, job seekers are even able to catalyze an organization into creating a new job for them by describing and substantiating the added value of their potential contribution to the organization.

Evaluate relative power realistically. Know when to push your agenda, when to concede a point, and when to table an issue for future discussion.

Do you have other opportunities or job offers in the wings? What are the unique skills and abilities you bring to the table? Are there other qualified candidates for the position? What resources do you have available? How risky is accepting the job? Are you giving up a degree of security professionally or financially in exchange for this opportunity?

FROM THE EMPLOYER'S SIDE OF THE TABLE

Historically, relative power has been weighted on the side of the employer, but in a tight labor market it is more equally distributed. If a worker or a potential employee has skills that are in high demand, and the company's need for such skills is urgent, a successful outcome to the negotiation relies on your willingness and ability to approach the negotiations with an open mind. On the other hand, in a period of abundant labor resources and multiple qualified job candidates, the need to offer flexibility is reduced.

POINTS TO REMEMBER
- Relative power is an essential intuitive concept in negotiations.
- A number of business climate, company, and individual factors influence relative power.
- Assessing your relative power is a critical step in realistic preparation for negotiations.
- Individuals with initiative and business savvy can actively shape the conditions of their employment.

RELATIVE POWER WORKSHEET

Use the following worksheet to assess the employer's circumstances and flexibility in relation to your own opportunities, unique skills, and resources; the competition; and your career objectives.

In the **Negotiable Element** column, list each component of the job offer. Under **Business Climate**, consider factors such as the economy, the industry, the unemployment rate, and the demand for skills and knowledge. Under **Worker Relative Power**, consider the other opportunities available to you, your own unique skills and knowledge, your competition for the job, and how the job fits into your overall career goals. In the **Employer Flexibility** column, consider the company's profitability and place in the business cycle, its urgency to fill the position, and the decision-making authority and staffing budget of the person with whom you are negotiating. Under **Notes**, list your other thoughts and observations. The first row shows a sample entry.

NEGOTIABLE ELEMENT	BUSINESS CLIMATE	WORKER RELATIVE POWER	EMPLOYER FLEXIBILITY	NOTES
Job content	Good economy Low unemployment	Current skills in demand; good rapport established with hiring manager, who appears to have the authority to make decisions about staff development	Small company; management fairly flexible; jobs very broadly defined	It is important to me that my job include cross-training and further skill-development opportunities. Based on my observations, it is likely that management would entertain my proposal.

continues

continued

NEGOTIABLE ELEMENT	BUSINESS CLIMATE	WORKER RELATIVE POWER	EMPLOYER FLEXIBILITY	NOTES

PART II

The Organizational Context

This section deals with the contributions workers make to the success of organizations. It also helps you assess the characteristics of employing organizations—the theatres in which work is performed.

CHAPTER 3

People—
The Competitive Advantage

NEGOTIATION VIEWPOINT

First and foremost, organizations need the right people. Time, technology, and capital are finite; it is the knowledge and strengths of its *human* resources—its people—that make the critical difference, that enable a business to succeed. Organizations are energized by the sum of the unique and specialized contributions of their employees.

WHAT IS THE COMPETITIVE ADVANTAGE ALL ABOUT?

It is a widely recognized business tenet that a company's people are its most important asset. Only people can bring about—or resist—change. Ideally, the company should enable employees to realize their potential and creative capacity. By doing so, not only does the organization benefit from higher productivity, but workers are fulfilled personally.

HOW DOES THE COMPETITIVE ADVANTAGE AFFECT YOU?

Working toward the best possible use of talents is in both the employee's and the organization's best interests.

We are all alike in that we are all different. Knowing ourselves and recognizing the added value we bring to the organization in the form of knowledge, skills, abilities, experience, and education is important. At every level, employees value being treated with respect, knowing how they are helping the company meet its goals, and having their contributions to that effort acknowledged.

FROM THE EMPLOYER'S SIDE OF THE TABLE

Employers today recognize that the contributions of their people make or break a business. What are some of the ways in which your workforce makes a critical difference to the success of your business? What programs does the organization have to recognize and develop its people? How are employees valued at the company? How is the company positioned with regard to encouraging and maximizing the potential of its workforce? How is the organization growing or changing? What kind of skills and abilities will you need to have in place in the future? The answers to these broad questions describe the organizational context for your hiring decisions.

POINTS TO REMEMBER

- ◆ People make the difference in enabling an organization to achieve its goals.

- ◆ Enlightened organizations recognize the importance of having an appropriately skilled workforce.

- ◆ As a skilled employee, you will make a positive contribution to an organization's competitive edge.

- ◆ Preparing for future human resource needs in alignment with anticipated change and growth is an important part of a company's organizational planning.

COMPETITIVE ADVANTAGE
SUMMARY WORKSHEET

Review and summarize the combination of specialized knowledge, skills, and abilities that made you the standout candidate for the job. Look over your resume for specific strengths to emphasize during the negotiation. These will form the solid foundation of added value upon which you can build your negotiation strategy.

KNOWLEDGE:

SKILLS:

ABILITIES/TALENTS:

EXPERIENCE:

EDUCATION:

CHAPTER 4

The Employment Environment

NEGOTIATION VIEWPOINT

The employment environment is a marketplace for monetary and nonmonetary exchange. The availability of other qualified candidates and the demand for up-to-date knowledge and skills directly affect job-offer negotiations. Priorities and resources vary widely among organizations and potential employees. Almost by definition, every aspect of the contract between an employer and an employee is potentially negotiable.

Due to both internal and external pressures, the business climate and the occupational environment—the context within which we work—is changing rapidly from an orientation of manufacturing and production to one of information management and service. Within companies, cost efficiencies, changing workforce values, and the continuing need for brand new or updated skills create different workplace requirements. Outside companies, the twenty-first century's worldwide marketplace brings additional competition, while government legislation and industry regulations and standards demand added compliance and vigilance. Mergers and acquisitions that dramatically change the business landscape are becoming the norm.

The nature of the work being performed in the future will lead to the development of situation-specific jobs. In response to change, organizations will reinvent and recombine work and job functions. An accountant who in the past applied traditional accounting knowledge in predictable, cyclical processes may need to refocus and work with an outside vendor to assess and put a new accounting system in place, or attend to the challenging task of bringing a company public.

WHAT IS THE EMPLOYMENT ENVIRONMENT ALL ABOUT?

The employment environment is evolving from a paternalistic workplace, in which most decisions were made for employees, to a partnership between the employer and employee. New values of open communication, cooperation, and shared responsibility are emerging as a result of the need to balance the many tensions affecting employment today.

With the dissolution of the paternalistic system also comes the disappearance of absolute loyalty in both directions. Workers cannot expect to be guaranteed a job forever. In parallel, employers cannot expect employees to stay with the company for their entire careers.

The organization identifies profit objectives and the human resources needed to support the achievement of those targets. By working together to match organizational and employee needs and goals and to maximize career opportunity, both employer and employee benefit.

HOW DOES THE EMPLOYMENT ENVIRONMENT AFFECT YOU?

Employees will continue to be more and more self-directed. People will need initiative and innovative thinking to establish, advance, and maintain careers, and to develop new careers, adapting to changes in employment opportunities.

With the renewed emphasis on self-responsibility comes the need to take charge of your own career development. The new employment paradigm will encourage workers to broaden and enhance their knowledge and skills.

We must understand the work environment and the forces impacting it in order to identify ways we can add value to a company and make a good job fit. Where do you want to be in five years? Ten? What resources will you need, and what factors will influence your ability to get there? Plan accordingly!

FROM THE EMPLOYER'S SIDE OF THE TABLE

It seems as though employers, reading and reacting to continued change and heightened competition, must juggle more unknowns than ever before. The ever-increasing pace of change has greatly added to the complexity of the business environment. Unlike the relatively slow growth of the past, when the nature of work was often stable over a period of years, change can be expected to continue accelerating. Keeping abreast of relevant change and anticipating trends will help to maintain a responsive work environment in which employees will be productive.

POINTS TO REMEMBER

- The employment picture is no longer one of paternalism but one of partnership.

- Lifetime careers with one employer are no longer the rule or the expectation.

- Many forces, both internal and external, put pressure on the work environment.

- We need to understand these pressures in order to find our "fit" and manage our careers.

TIPS ON THE EMPLOYMENT ENVIRONMENT

External Forces

Every business and occupation today is constantly being reshaped. Global competition and economic realities, political events, legal and regulatory requirements, and exploding technology all exert strong influence on the economics of business. As we progress into the twenty-first century, we can expect to continue adapting our work structure to the effects of change. Can you imagine using the limited computer capabilities that were state-of-the-art only a few computer "generations" ago and conducting business competitively under those circumstances today?

The Nature of Work

The rate of technology development and product change is exponential. This change continues to redefine the nature of the work being performed. Going forward, job responsibilities will be reconfigured more and more frequently, requiring a much more broadly skilled and flexible workforce than in the past.

The Organization of the Future

In the future, organizations may polarize into core and noncore employment. Core employees will be those whose knowledge differentiates the organization—management and those engaged in the development and income-producing aspects of the work. In this scenario, core employees possibly will make up less than half of a company's total workforce. The noncore majority will be made up of two segments: contingent "just-in-time" jobs, and long-term professional-level people who will staff the support areas that don't directly generate income.

Contingent employment is work dictated by the need for labor—a just-in-time employment adjustment to economic shifts. Contingent employment enables a company to temporarily increase staffing during peak periods. This trend toward outsourcing noncore work has given a boost to the growth of Professional Employer Organizations (PEOs), companies that provide human-resource expertise, payroll services, and benefits administration to customer companies.

Employee leasing is a work arrangement in which workers are actually employed by a third-party administrator that handles payroll, benefits, and human-resources functions for a fee, while the serviced company directs the work that the employees perform. *Interim workers* are those in higher-level salaried professional positions of limited duration. *Temporary employees* are hired for short-term assignments; "temps" are often hired and placed through an outside temporary employment agency.

These and other nonstandard employment arrangements are outlined in the following table:

Nonstandard/Alternative Employment Arrangements

WORKER TYPE	NATURE OF EMPLOYMENT
Intern, co-op, work-study	High school and college student employment that combines work and educational advancement
Temporary	An hourly worker, hired ad hoc for a specific job with an end date, who is paid by the temporary agency
Temp-to-hire	Hourly, converts to regular after a period of time during which the company and employee are looking each other over, similar in a sense to a probationary period
Leased	An employee of a leasing company who receives an annualized salary with benefits, regardless of whether he or she is currently placed with a client company
Interim	A higher-level professional position of less than one year duration; salaried
Contingent	A short-term employee, generally hired for one year or less, with no implicit or explicit contract for ongoing employment (excludes students, retirees)
Contract	A worker/service provided to another company at their work site for an hourly or fixed rate for the specified length of the project
Subcontractor	A worker paid by a general contractor on behalf of the client company
Per diem	A worker that receives a lump sum or fixed price; paid per day
On-call/ day labor	A pool of workers who are called to work as needed
Consultant	A highly compensated professional possessing a specialized body of knowledge; generally receives no client company group benefits
Self-employed, independent contractor, freelance work	A worker who provides a product or service to his or her own customers; engaged for a specified task generally not performed by regular company employees and for a limited time period

The Employment Covenant

The unspoken understanding between employer and employee has changed. No longer is lifetime employment an implicit promise in exchange for worker loyalty. Today, workers are beginning to view themselves as entrepreneurs and independent contractors within the larger employment environment. People are taking pride in and making commitments to their professions, their jobs, and themselves, rather than to a single employer.

Worker Demographics

The makeup of the workforce continues to evolve, with more women developing high-profile careers and more members of minority groups coming into their own. Another factor is the maturing of the influential "baby boomer" population segment. Among many other characteristics, employees differ by race, color, religion, gender, national origin, and age. Cultural diversity is a natural attribute of this new worker mix and of the customers that most businesses seek to serve. The general understanding of diversity has expanded to accepting the differences and valuing the contributions of all segments of the working population.

The Americans with Disabilities Act (ADA) established a baseline of reasonable accommodation for disabled workers capable of performing essential job functions. The availability of assistance devices at affordable cost makes it easier for those with motor, sensory, or neurological impairments to enjoy new job opportunities in the workplace.

Career Development

A career can be described as a progression of work-related experiences. In the broadest sense, it is the making of a contribution over time. Careers and career subsets progress through a sequence: development, establishment, plateau, and mentoring. Our personal likes and dislikes influence our career choices, and our needs and goals can be expected to shift somewhat as we move through career and life-cycle stages.

CHAPTER 5

The Organization

NEGOTIATION VIEWPOINT

In evaluating a job offer and preparing to negotiate terms of employment, you must be familiar with the organization as a business entity and a system. The organization is the theatre for the negotiation and you must adapt the negotiation to it.

Organizations are formed by a vision and governed by a mission that owners and management want to achieve. Organizations are distinguished by their culture, structure, management style, and communications practices.

WHAT IS THE ORGANIZATION ALL ABOUT?

Every organization is involved in developing, making, packaging, selling, and distributing its product or service, whether tangible or intangible, for defined purposes. Based on product and purpose, organizations are often categorized as being for-profit or nonprofit.

Organizations are dynamic market- and customer-driven entities made up of clusters of work functions that either directly generate product and income or support production. Organizations are macrosystems; that is, they require input, process that input, and produce output. Within the overall system are multiple microsystems, an arrangement of inter-dependent, related inputs, processes, and outputs.

Output may be manufacturing-based or information- and knowledge-based. Every successful organization functions with the interests of its constituencies in mind—customers, employees, share or interest holders, and to a certain extent, vendors and suppliers.

HOW DOES THE ORGANIZATION AFFECT YOU?

Organizational input, or resources, include raw materials, capital, technology (including methods and procedures), and people—people with knowledge, skills, and abilities to contribute to, and with roles to perform in, the organizational system. To become and remain successful, every organization must constantly balance between controlling and coordinating its component systems and functions and being flexible. Flexibility is required to create and maintain an environment in which workers will thrive and contribute optimally toward business goals.

The way an organization functions, the way it is structured, the way it is managed, and the way employees communicate with one another all affect whether you will do well there. These characteristics will also influence how able the company will be to meet your needs during negotiations.

FROM THE EMPLOYER'S SIDE OF THE TABLE

The organization is a collection of subsystems of work functions that are developed around its product(s). These subsystems include materials, capital, technology, and staffing. The organization's persona is defined through its culture, structure, management style, and communications habits. No one element can be viewed in isolation from the others.

The culture of your organization is a subtle (or not so subtle) understanding about "how things are done in the company," sometimes guided by a code of conduct statement or an employee manual, but more often simply translated in the way people view their engagement in the work of your organization.

The structure of an organization is usually carefully planned and aimed at achieving the organization's goals as efficiently as possible. Many employers find that traditional, authority-based structures are easier to manage. Others are recognizing that although they have less direct control, matrixed and participative work environments are more productive and innovative.

Matrixed work involves multiple group memberships for jobs, with workers handling somewhat different responsibilities depending on a particular group's makeup and focus. It highlights team leadership skills and the ability to manage work relationships. In a large, structured organization there is likely to be less autonomy to conduct offer negotiations, and the degree of freedom that does exist will probably be more carefully defined.

Organizations set out their management methodologies—rule-bound or relaxed, controlling or enabling. Within these general practices, managers develop their own style of managing. Whether a manager's work values are primarily results-oriented, more relationship-driven, or some combination thereof will form the basis for his or her approach to management.

The way you convey a job offer to a potential employee will reflect your own way of communicating and that of the organization. A reserved, carefully composed offer, which implies little leeway or tolerance for negotiation, may indicate traditional—centralized, prescribed, or directed—organizational communications. A more casually worded offer, with room to explore the possibilities and consequences of various work arrangements, would be more characteristic of open, reciprocal, and dynamic communications.

POINTS TO REMEMBER

- Organizations form the architecture for the arrangement of the work you will be doing.

- Organizations are systems that are made up of many contributing subsystems.

- Large or small, for-profit or nonprofit, organizations are molded by the need to balance control and flexibility.

- Aspects of the organization with which you should become familiar are its culture, structure, management style, and organizational communications.

ORGANIZATIONAL CULTURE

In evaluating a job offer and preparing to negotiate terms of employment, finding a comfort level with the organization's philosophy and culture is an important first step. To some extent, organizational culture is an indicator of what parts of the job offer may or may not be negotiable. For example, in discussing work arrangements at an organization known for routinely long workdays, expressing an interest in a flexible schedule might be negatively viewed as indicating a lack of commitment to the job. (The cultural "schedule" may be to come in early and work late.)

The culture of an organization is largely abstract, supported by stories and myths that create a way of looking at its people and events. Organizational culture is embodied in its leadership. Although it does evolve in reaction to its internal and external environments, culture is slow to change.

WHAT IS ORGANIZATIONAL CULTURE ALL ABOUT?

Organizational culture is a complexity that develops around "the way we do things" within a company. Essentially, it is the nature and identity of an organization. Culture is made up of taken-for-granted assumptions, expectations, and sometimes misconceptions. It is made up of an organization's shared values and meanings, exhibited through ways of doing the work of the business. A company's culture is a central set of beliefs that provide the rationale for a particular view and orientation toward work and ways of behaving within the organizational setting.

The company's geographic location, its presence in the community, union or nonunion status, and any special interests contribute to the definition of its culture. Indicators of the culture include the degree of flexibility offered—is it a one-size-fits-all concept? Individual and group demographics, such as the mix between younger and older employees, singles and families, may be representative of the culture. The professional-technical-clerical composition, aggregates of short- and long-term worker service length, and overall level of employee education are factors contributing to the company's workforce profile. To a large extent, an organization's culture may be reflected in its diversity.

HOW DOES ORGANIZATIONAL CULTURE AFFECT YOU?

People often identify with an organization most strongly through its culture. Culture is the backdrop for the work performed in an organization. It sets the course—formal or informal, isolated or supportive, risk-averse or entrepreneurial—of the organization.

Before evaluating the design of the job and the compensation and benefits being offered, look once more at the employing organization itself. Is the organization's philosophy and culture a comfortable operating climate for you?

You can tell a lot about an organization just by looking around outside at the buildings, grounds, landscaping and maintenance, and parking. Inside, are visitors welcomed and made comfortable in a reception area? Within the corridors and work areas, what is the level of activity? Is it quiet or noisy? How is the workspace designed? Is it well appointed, well equipped, and well lit? What is the style of office furniture? Are the materials, tools, and resources you need to do your work readily available? Do people wear business attire or dress casually? Is there a smoking policy? Are there other observable social or behavioral mores? How does this organization compare with others in the same industry or field?

Companies often explain their organizational philosophy in their corporate vision, their values commitment (which states "how we work"), or the corporate mission statement (which states "why we work"). Will this philosophy accommodate your values and personal work environment preferences—your employment likes and dislikes?

You will have formed an impression of the organization's culture during earlier interviews. Take the time to confirm your impressions and be sure you can comfortably fit in. The current climate of the organization will greatly influence how easily you will be able to make innovations in, and exercise choices about, your work.

FROM THE EMPLOYER'S SIDE OF THE TABLE

Your company's culture is manifested by how business is conducted and the way in which work is accomplished. The business culture directly interconnects with an employee's personal work philosophy and values.

You undoubtedly gauged a prospective employee's comfort with the organization's culture during the interview phase, and you will reinforce your impression of the candidate's cultural compatibility as you negotiate the job offer. It goes without saying that to earn worker buy-in and trust, the overriding vision and espoused philosophy of the company must be seamlessly integrated with actual business practice.

POINTS TO REMEMBER

- Organizational culture is about "how we do things."

- The culture of an organization is constantly evolving, shaped by both management and employee beliefs.

- An organization's culture provides a cue for assessing your fit within the organization and what components of the job offer may be negotiable.

ORGANIZATIONAL STRUCTURE

The structure of an organization and the way it makes decisions will directly bias what may be negotiable and with whom you must undertake the negotiations in order for them to be productive.

Business strategy and planning strongly influence an organization's infrastructure—traditionally hierarchical or partnership oriented, rigidly constructed or modular. The structure of a business is often expressive of leadership's management philosophy and shaped by the size of the company, the nature of its products, its target markets and customers, and the geographic regions it serves.

WHAT IS ORGANIZATIONAL STRUCTURE ALL ABOUT?

An organization's structure may be centralized (often using a rigid chain-of-command and hierarchical approach), or matrixed, containing multiple job and work relationships. Matrixed (dimensional) organizations are characterized by linchpin worker links that help manage the interdependence of departments. The trend today is toward the latter: decentralized, "organic" organizations with many dotted-line reporting relationships that encourage collaborative problem solving. Organizations generally are segmented by functionality, by geographic area, or by product lines—an arrangement that may result in a duplication of support functions.

HOW DOES ORGANIZATIONAL STRUCTURE AFFECT YOU?

The organization is a dynamic system composed of interacting variables, each working with input and output from other systems. People are integral to the system. Each system functions within a defined external environment and embodies the knowledge, skills, and abilities of its employees, as well as the nature of its work and its supporting technology.

The structure of an organization includes the ways in which people are grouped to perform work. Traditional organizations often cluster workers based on profession and tenure. Many organizations now have interdisciplinary, cross-functional, or process teams focused on putting out a quality product efficiently or implementing cost savings. Startup venture and network organizations may essentially have one band of employees who work together on phased implementations, motivated by profit-sharing incentives.

Organizational structure is the set upon which work is performed. It shapes the way work is performed, prescribes job definition to some extent, and affects the significance of interdepartmental worker relationships. A traditional structure may indicate clearly defined job duties, with little room for alternative design; whereas in a matrixed organization, job content is more likely to be continually adapting.

FROM THE EMPLOYER'S SIDE OF THE TABLE

The manner in which a business is structured can govern what is negotiable and how much freedom a manager has to exercise independent judgment. If there is little tolerance or facility in the company for managing flexibility, the likelihood of working with an employee or a recruit to interpret the design, rewards, or conditions of a job may be reduced accordingly.

POINTS TO REMEMBER

- Organizational structure may be hierarchical or matrixed, and it represents management philosophy and business strategy.

- Decision-making may be chain-of-command or empowered.

- An organization's structure is often an indication of its flexibility, and as such it will have a direct bearing on the negotiation process.

- Organizational structure includes the way people are grouped to perform work.

MANAGEMENT STYLE

Management style is about an understanding of the notion of work. The way work is managed is changing fundamentally. Changing work patterns will, in turn, necessitate a more democratic type of management than was common in the past, one that is founded on interpersonal communications. Negotiation planning must consider the overall management style of the organization, but job-offer negotiations will be most directly impacted by management practice at the levels to which the open position will directly and indirectly report.

Often an outgrowth of organizational culture and structure, but also a function of the individual involved, management style both broadly reflects and closely sets the climate and parameters of the environment in which we work on a daily basis.

WHAT IS MANAGEMENT STYLE ALL ABOUT?

Most often, management style is an intertwining of organizational leadership custom and individual personality. In many organizations, management's role is moving away from authoritarian decision-making within a pyramid structure that emphasizes results monitoring. The new manager is a leader, coach, mentor, and liaison across fluid organizational boundaries.

HOW DOES MANAGEMENT STYLE AFFECT YOU?

Today we all must be self-directed to a greater extent than ever before, managing ourselves, our resources, and our careers. In a sense, we are all managers of ourselves as entrepreneurs, possessing marketable business knowledge, skills, and abilities.

It's important to understand a company's particular management style to negotiate with its representatives successfully. Whether leadership is centralized or decentralized, layers of management and the degree of monitoring and control through support areas suggest an organization's overall orientation to a style of management. Locally, a manager's span of control and the presence or absence of functional and project teams in the work environment further indicate whether management is bounded or matrixed.

A good grasp of the management style of both the company and the manager will help you plan your negotiation strategy. If a company's management is centralized or highly controlling, you will need to broach negotiations cautiously. Strategy here might be to pay your respects to the organization's authoritative management approach up front and acknowledge that this may make it more difficult initially to identify areas of flexibility. If the management of an organization is team-oriented, on the other hand, a negotiating strategy emphasizing openness and communications might be most productive. With the recent trend toward managers acting as facilitators who provide guidance and resources to get the work done, negotiating job variables may become a more commonly accepted practice.

A manager's particular problem-solving preferences—whether action- and results-focused, theoretical and forward thinking, cautious and thoughtful, or cooperative and concerned for others—reflect the management style with which an employee will most closely interact. Through self-assessment and experience, you will have become acquainted with your own inclinations and know whether you work best with a relatively high emphasis on task and accomplishment, or in an environment geared more toward teamwork, where relationships carry relatively greater weight.

A company's management practices are a significant factor in whether you would be comfortable and successful working there. Individual work performance and satisfaction are strongly influenced by a manager's style, coaching, and communications skills. Management preferences set the tone of the immediate environment within which a position functions.

FROM THE EMPLOYER'S SIDE OF THE TABLE

Hiring managers should be well versed in the various styles and shades of management types, and in particular your company's conventions and your own way of managing. By fully appreciating these givens—both strengths and gaps—you will be better able to discover, explore, and assess a prospective employee's best fit in your own area. You will also be better positioned to predict a worker's potential and efficacy in performing duties that extend their responsibilities to coordinating and working with people in various other parts of the organization.

POINTS TO REMEMBER

- Management style is an outgrowth of both corporate and personal preferences.

- You must take management practice into consideration when planning your negotiation strategy.

- The work environment in which an individual functions is directly impacted by management style.

TIPS ON MANAGEMENT STYLE

A number of indicators can help you identify a manager's values and preferred way of working. Gaining insight into management style can help you decide whether you can work comfortably with an individual. Style assessment also provides information for framing your approach to the job-offer negotiation.

Task/Relationship Focus

You can infer management style from the relative value a person places on task accomplishment and relationship maintenance and how an individual frames his or her conversations, as well as from references relative to their general work focus and perspective:

Perspective-Focus Grid

Sensing	**Intuiting**
Outlook Present	*Outlook Future*
Focus: immediate action	Focus: long range, big picture
Style: challenge-oriented, problem-solving	Style: conceptual, theoretical
Thinking	**Feeling**
Outlook Progression	*Outlook Past*
Focus: organization and analysis	Focus: relationships
Style: logical, systematic	Style: empathetic, cooperative, conventional

The style analysis shown here is based on preference identification theory developed by Carl Jung, as interpreted, adapted, and popularized by Myers-Briggs and others. It is meaningful in that we all have our own way of viewing work and work focus, preferences that fall somewhere within and between the four quadrants, some of which are more compatible with specific management styles than others.

Do you know where your own work style would be plotted on the perspective-focus grid? How does each operating style as outlined in the grid fit with your own view of work?

Direct Inquiries into Management Style

Another way to identify management preference is simply to ask questions and evaluate the answers during the interview process. This is the most practical method for a job seeker attempting to evaluate the management style of a potential employer. Sample questions might be the following:

- ◆ What is your approach to management?
- ◆ What work style do you look for in members of your team?
- ◆ How do you ensure achievement of your objectives?
- ◆ How do you handle a crisis?
- ◆ How do you view work/family issues?
- ◆ What is the turnover experience here and why is this position open?
- ◆ How, and how often, do you communicate with your people?
- ◆ How, and how often, do you provide performance feedback to your staff?
- ◆ What work-related qualities do you most value in your staff?

Look for open and honest replies, ask for examples or clarification if necessary, and *read the manager's body language.*

ORGANIZATIONAL COMMUNICATION

Communication characteristics are evident both in a company's business publications and in its routine ways of conveying information internally. The mode of communication surrounding career exploration discussions and a job offer establishes convention and sets the tone for the negotiations script.

Communication roles, vehicles, networks, messages, and the degree of openness all articulate an employer's way of communicating. Organizational communications are a component of the organizational persona and a strong indicator of the nature of the work environment.

WHAT IS ORGANIZATIONAL COMMUNICATION ALL ABOUT?

Organizational communication—the control, coordination, and dissemination, and the degree of sharing of information—runs along a continuum from stable and directive to dynamic. In centralized, highly structured organizations, decisions are made at the top and communications occur through concrete channels, with information cascading and filtering down through the organizational pyramid only when and to the extent that it is intended. Standardization and rules about correct and incorrect actions and decisions and prescribed ways of doing things set limits. Procedures are often ordered and rote. Information hoarding may be an unrecognized barrier to workflow. In such organizations, employees often view the rumor mill and grapevine as more reliable than authorized or management-endorsed communication.

In decentralized or dimensional organizations, decisions are shared and made at all organizational levels. Even more critical, communication occurs constantly, using both formal and unofficial channels for information sharing. Information flow and coordination between departments and functional and support areas is essential. The need for reciprocal communication is heightened by the trend toward shared resources and functional and project teams that are focused on efficiency and responsiveness. Communication skills and candor are important assets for every employee in this type of organization.

HOW DOES ORGANIZATIONAL COMMUNICATION AFFECT YOU?

Like management style, organizational communications offer significant clues to a company's personality. Is communication top-down and dictatorial, or bottom-up and strongly influenced by employees? Does centralized communication take place in a "stovepipe"—one-way down and/or up? Or is communication decentralized, occurring across a web— between suborganizational business units and disciplines and freely among individuals at all levels? The way in which your job offer is communicated— whether it is made in person, conveyed over the telephone, or confirmed in writing—may be an indication of a company's communications practices. If the offer is formal, carefully worded, and crisp (brisk, matter-of-fact, and to the point), its terms are likely to be fairly rigid. If the offer is presented in a more casual manner initially, inviting discussion, there may be more room for negotiation.

Are you comfortable in a structured setting, knowing basically "what to do and how to do it," and working with information provided on a need-to-know basis? Or do you prefer to see the larger picture and the interconnection of the elements of business? Do you view knowledge and information as part of your power base, or do you openly and readily share your knowledge and expertise with others? The communication network of an organization is an observable phenomenon, representative of the atmosphere in which you will work.

FROM THE EMPLOYER'S SIDE OF THE TABLE

By structuring the interview process along the lines of the organization's communication model, you will have a good sense of the prospective employee's interactive predisposition. Since communication is the basis for direction and interaction, understanding and rapport is essential for a positive outcome to the job offer negotiations presently on the table, and ultimately, to a successful working relationship.

POINTS TO REMEMBER

- Communication practices are a visible indicator of an employer's culture, structure, and management strategy.

- Communication skills and candor are highly valued in dimensional organizations.

- The manner in which a job offer is conveyed will often set the interactive tone of the negotiation.

ORGANIZATIONAL ANALYSIS WORKSHEET

Think back over the observations you have made in working with the employing organization thus far. What assumptions can you make about its culture, structure, management style, and communications? Use the following worksheet (or your own version based on this one) to list your impressions regarding the many aspects of the organization: culture, structure, management style, and communications.

CULTURE
STRUCTURE
MANAGEMENT STYLE
COMMUNICATIONS

PART III

The Negotiation Process

This section provides an in-depth look at negotiations as a methodology made up of two fundamental operations: planning and communication.

CHAPTER 6

Managing the Negotiation Project

NEGOTIATION VIEWPOINT

You can manage any negotiation most effectively by identifying your needs and interests *and* the needs and interests of the other party, and by looking for ways to satisfy both entities.

Negotiation is the structuring of an exchange or transaction—give and get. It is often a process of compromise over time, in which the interested parties reach or renew agreement on the terms and conditions of the relationship.

WHAT IS MANAGING THE NEGOTIATION PROJECT ALL ABOUT?

Negotiation takes place in two distinct, equally important phases: **preparation** and **communication**. Preparation includes research, planning, and strategy beforehand; communication encompasses information interchange and agreement at the negotiation itself.

Negotiation requires **project management** expertise. Project management involves identifying, marshaling, and making the best use of resources to achieve a specific objective.

In addition to the ability to manage a project, skills for successful negotiation include data gathering and analysis, interpersonal and communications skills, and the ability to think inclusively.

The timing of the actual negotiation discussion is critical. The best time to negotiate is *after* a serious job offer has been made and *before* you have fully accepted it. When an offer is extended, the employer has made the decision that you are the qualified recruit best suited for the job. You are interested, but you may still be evaluating all of the opportunities available to you. You have not yet made a commitment. It is at this juncture that you have the most bargaining leverage.

HOW DOES MANAGING THE NEGOTIATION PROJECT AFFECT YOU?

Once the initial offer parameters are fully stated, express interest and enthusiasm and then ask for time to consider the job offer, framing your request in light of the importance of the decision. This creates a brief period of time in which to prepare for negotiating the employment covenant, the final design of the job itself, compensation and benefits, and job perks. It is probable that you will have given some preliminary thought to each of these areas, so you may already have a good general sense of what compensation and benefits you can expect and how much you really want the job.

Sometimes it is possible to split the negotiation into two pieces—reviewing and firming up job design and content when the offer is made and then dealing with compensation and benefits at a later meeting. In such an instance, don't lose sight of the cardinal rule regarding a job offer: Take some time to think about the offer—*don't make an impulsive decision.*

The negotiation project is an opportunity to define, convey, and obtain what you want with regard to the terms and conditions of the job. Be sure you are familiar with all relevant data sources—those containing the information that will help you plan the negotiation.

The closer your interests are aligned with those of the company, the greater the likelihood of a mutually satisfactory, successful outcome to negotiations. And how definitively the final offer matches what you want may be an indication of both the influence you will hold in the new position and the authority the hiring manager has to meet staff human-resource needs.

FROM THE EMPLOYER'S SIDE OF THE TABLE

Negotiation is usually the final step, with the possible exceptions of reference checking and testing/medical screening, in the hiring process. Having found a top-notch candidate, you are invested in guiding the negotiations to the desired wrap-up. Most recruiters and hiring managers are willing to tackle job negotiations, once the outstanding applicant has been identified and selected, and after the individual's level of interest in the job has been ascertained. Today, many employees expect to take an active role in crafting working agreements. By creating a climate of discussion throughout the interview period, you have already sounded out and gained an initial sense of an interviewee's concerns prior to approaching this last hurdle. Your understanding of the prospective employee's interests will help you to structure the most persuasive approach to the job offer and negotiation process.

POINTS TO REMEMBER

* Approach the negotiation as a project to be managed.

* The negotiation process involves preparation and communication.

* The timing of negotiations is critical to a successful outcome.

CHAPTER 7

Phase I: Preparation

NEGOTIATION VIEWPOINT

Once you have secured a job offer, carefully consider what is being proposed. You and the employer may have different needs, interests, and values. Prepare yourself to respond comfortably to a rather natural employer bias. The employer may be inclined to see things only from the company's vantage point; for example, a hiring manager may at first react abruptly to a candidate's proposal with "We don't have the expertise to do that here" or "Nobody offers that benefit," unaware of the outside resources that are available or accepted practice elsewhere.

Preparation includes research, planning, and strategizing your response, knowing your own needs and interests, and anticipating your prospective employer's needs and interests. Remember, make no commitment on the spot when a job offer is extended. Be prepared to ask for time to consider the offer, no matter how attractive it may seem. Be sure to request the company's benefits handbook to review while you are evaluating the offer.

RESEARCH

WHAT IS RESEARCH ALL ABOUT?

Research is gathering pertinent information—knowing what information to collect. Research also includes filtering—selecting the information that is most relevant to the situation. In the evaluation of a job offer, research involves gaining familiarity with the larger employment context and external influences on the business, the employer, and oneself. See the big picture and the whole picture—economy, industry, location, job market, company, profession, job, and individual.

Know the employer—in preparation for employment interviews, you collected information on the employing company. Look back again at the business environment within which the employer operates. A trip online or to the library will yield a wealth of resource materials—directories, references, business magazines, and newspapers. Research the employer through trade publications. Review the company's annual report, 10K report (filed with the Securities and Exchange Commission), and proxy statements. Request and read a comprehensive benefits booklet from the employer; and talk to your accountant or refer to applicable Internal Revenue Service publications to assess the tax aspects of the benefits package.

Think about the negotiation from the employer's standpoint. Identify the employer's probable issues, gauge the employer's position, and anticipate the employer's arguments. Then, research and be able to articulate the implications of the issues from a business, as well as a human, perspective. Script your proposals, practice responding verbally with a tape recorder, or even use videotape to perfect your presentation.

A company's latitude to negotiate employment terms varies. Smaller companies may have fewer rules and regulations but may be correspondingly less familiar with possibilities. Larger, more bureaucratic organizations may be less flexible. Unionized environments are highly structured and usually have little if any tolerance for individually negotiated situations. Be sure to understand what constraints may exist—specific conditions that will impact the negotiation.

HOW DOES RESEARCH AFFECT YOU?

Know yourself. Early in your job search, or perhaps in considering unsolicited career opportunities, you developed an image of the job you wanted: industry, location, company, job, salary, and so forth. This same thought process forms the basis for negotiating a job offer. Knowing yourself—who you are professionally, what you have to offer, and what and where you want to be—is your touchstone throughout the negotiation process.

Establish negotiation objectives with an eye to reality, keeping in mind your short- and long-term goals and desired outcomes. Ask yourself, "What are my interests?" "What do I want to achieve?" "What are the logical steps?" "What can I influence?" Consider psychic income as well as financial opportunity. Will the job require and reward your strengths?

Then prioritize, "What is critical?" "What do I value?" "What will meet my needs?" Identify opportunities for compromise: "What can I give up to get what I want?" Know what is of low cost to you but of high benefit to the employer (and vice versa), and know your best alternative—the better and more well thought-out your options, the greater your confidence level. Having more than one option is a significant source of power in any negotiation.

Ask yourself what personal resources you can use in the negotiation. In some ways, negotiating skills are an extension of interviewing skills, incorporating an ability you already refined in obtaining the offer. A quick review of interviewing techniques can help you prepare for the negotiation. In fact, the interview may have presented the first opportunity for you to begin subtle communication of what is important to you: "ballpark" (general) salary range expectations, past benefits, and benefit concerns. Make the assumption throughout your interviewing experience that negotiations will be a part of the hiring process.

FROM THE EMPLOYER'S SIDE OF THE TABLE

Large corporations often have greater breadth and depth of established benefits components with which to work, while smaller and midsize companies probably have more flexibility but are generally dealing with less precedent and fewer program dollars.

Consider labor supply and demand and the resultant relative power, and the balance of time, capital, technology, people, ideas, products, and expertise. Know what is highly prized by the potential employee and look at the ways in which you may have the ability to meet that need. During the interview period you established credibility and began building a relationship with the recruit. Recognize that negotiation is a legitimate part of forging a working agreement. Be able to look at the issues from a human, and humane, standpoint. Think about the negotiation from the candidate's perspective. Identify probable concerns and be open to and prepared to respond to the information that the candidate may present in support of a proposal.

Know where there is room for flexibility and where there is little or none. However, be extremely wary of interpreting benefits programs in specific individual situations without first consulting with appropriate expert resources. Be thoroughly familiar with, and prepared to discuss, current organizational practices and programs in place with regard to the following items:

- personnel policies and procedures
- the selection process
- training and development
- performance management
- compensation: base pay program, short-term incentive, long-term incentive, and benefits, including

    medical and dental coverage

    income protection

    relocation programs

    retirement plans and termination practices

    work and family programs

    entertainment, travel and expense reimbursement

    executive benefits

    safety
- other company- and job-specific aspects of employment.

POINTS TO REMEMBER

- ◆ Negotiation requires preparatory research.

- ◆ Research must include external influences on the business environment, as well as employer needs and interests.

- ◆ Research must also encompass a review of your strengths and identification of your short- and long-term goals.

TIPS ON RESEARCH

Use the following checklist to guide your research or to review and add to the information about the company that you gathered in preparation for earlier interviews.

Checklist: Researching a Prospective Employer

BUSINESS ENVIRONMENT AND ECONOMIC AND INDUSTRY TRENDS

☐ Climate of the external operating environment

☐ Industry competitors

☐ Organizational credentialing

☐ Reputation in industry

☐ Financial history

☐ Business milestones

☐ Annual report

☐ Revenues

☐ Primary functions

☐ Size

☐ Products, processes, equipment, and resources

CORPORATE CULTURE, STRUCTURE, AND MANAGEMENT STYLE

☐ History

☐ Philosophy and culture

☐ General short- and long-term business goals

☐ Centralized/decentralized organizational configuration

☐ Location(s)

☐ Formal/informal makeup and style of management

☐ Communications channels

☐ Key names, titles

Relate the previous research to your own strengths, weaknesses, and short- and long-term goals:

SUITABILITY: THE COMPANY'S MISSION AND GOALS

☐ What do you know about the company's mission and goals?

☐ Why are you interested in working for this company?

COMPATIBILITY: PERSONAL QUALITIES AND COMPANY CULTURE

☐ What is your preferred work environment?

☐ What is your own management style?

☐ How would you and your approach to work be described by your peers, colleagues, management, staff?

☐ How do you motivate others?

☐ If you encountered significant problems in this job, what would they likely be?

☐ How would you handle a situation in which you were required by your management to do something in a way that you thought was unproductive or inappropriate?

Personal Marketing Statement

Know yourself. Look back at the Competitive Advantage Summary Worksheet in part II or the marketing introduction you constructed as part of your interview preparation. Or you can create a summary of your experience, knowledge, skills, and abilities now using the following worksheet as an example. Always keep in mind where you would like to be three to five years down the road—your future work and life goals.

Personal Marketing Example (short description statement)

Interpersonal or background note: _____
_____.

PRODUCT/SERVICES (WHAT I AM)

I am an experienced _____ (occupation) with
expertise in _____ (area[s] of focus) *and/or*
I have a degree in _____ (educational background).

WORK HISTORY/ENVIRONMENT

Most recently I _____
_____
(accomplishments/client base).

SKILLS (WHAT I DO–PEOPLE, DATA, THINGS)

My strengths include _____
_____
(specific transferable skills).

TRAITS/INTERPERSONAL LINKAGE (WHO I AM–CHARACTERISTICS)

My areas of interest are _____
_____.

GOALS (WHAT I WANT)

My goals include _____
_____.

PLANNING

WHAT IS PLANNING ALL ABOUT?

Planning is about mentally setting the stage for negotiations. It is mapping out an approach, based on information you have gathered, to reach an objective. Planning is a detailed program of action.

Plan the negotiation. Be sure to be well informed, with both background information and thorough knowledge of the points to be discussed. Gather information about the environment in which the negotiation will occur: Know "who, what, when, where, why, and how":

+ With whom you will be negotiating

+ What you know about them and their personal style

+ When and where the negotiations will take place

+ Why you are negotiating—what you want—and how you will handle the discussions

Who you will be negotiating with affects your strategy. Try to confirm who has the authority to make and ratify the agreement. Look back at the "Management Style" section of chapter 5 and review how to identify this individual's style of management. Modify your approach accordingly.

Take the initiative. If you don't ask, you usually don't get. Keep in mind that a work agreement negotiation is not a zero-sum game. You are most directly affected by the outcome, but as an employee you must meet the needs of the company. Map the advantages and disadvantages of your proposals. Work on issue definition. Identify and analyze issues and develop ideas to defuse them. Document your position; support it by referencing common practice, precedents, or generally accepted standards. Prepare to counter resistance expressed as, "That's never been done before," or "We don't do that here," by researching and presenting solid supporting information on current trends.

Questions to ask yourself include:

+ What is the issue?

+ What is my position?

- Why? What is my rationale, my supporting resource, or my expertise?

- How will the employer view the issue?

    Anticipate objections.

    Formulate contingent "if-then" counters.

- What are the significant differences in the positions and how will I frame and convey my viewpoint?

Draft an agenda, but don't make it too rigid in case you have made erroneous assumptions. Unanticipated questions or responses will lead to frustration for a job candidate with an uncompromising and over-rehearsed agenda.

HOW DOES PLANNING AFFECT YOU?

We are all frequently involved in making plans and decisions in our personal lives. Our working lives too can be positively affected by advance planning. Planning for negotiation about the terms and conditions of work increases the likelihood of an enduring and mutually satisfactory work relationship.

Remember, job matching means identifying what the employer needs, wants, and values and identifying your corresponding personal and professional assets and qualifications. During the interview process, the employer evaluates a candidate's strengths as they relate to the needs of the business. This helps in predicting employee performance. In turn, you can link the offer negotiations to the job and to the added value you are bringing to the organization.

Needs are basic essentials for physical and psychological survival, such as food, shelter, and social interaction. Wants are wishes, usually defined as what we would like to have but can do without. Make sure you need or really want what you are negotiating for. Visualize yourself in your new position. Then do your homework and justify your proposals. By carefully planning the negotiation, you will have the quiet confidence you'll need to project in order to negotiate successfully.

FROM THE EMPLOYER'S SIDE OF THE TABLE

The planning required of the prospective employer, who is already familiar with the company's work environment, is usually less involved. Think back over past positive negotiated outcomes. Know what you have the authority to approve and who you need to confer with about exceptions.

An awareness of the recruit's personal style is helpful. While it is difficult to formulate an agenda outline for negotiations until you have first identified and then evaluated the issues being raised, anticipating the candidate's interests may be productive.

During the meeting, don't spend time responding to exploratory statements in generalities; be prepared to make unambiguous counters. Remember, empowered employees today are accustomed to being included in the process, to taking responsibility for themselves, and to having an active voice in their work environment. You have offered the position to the candidate who most closely meets the needs of the company. Predict the candidate's concerns, based on interviews and experience, then ask yourself:

- Is this an understandable concern? Why?

- Is this a deal-maker or deal-breaker issue?

- What is the company's position?

- What resources do I have to research this further?

- What authority and flexibility do I have, if any, to make a decision about this?

- Who is the final decision-maker?

- How can I counter the candidate's proposal with a more acceptable compromise?

POINTS TO REMEMBER

- ◆ Advance planning paves the way for successful negotiation.

- ◆ Identify and analyze potential issues.

- ◆ Know your priorities.

- ◆ Develop a rough agenda or outline for the negotiation.

- ◆ Maintain a positive attitude.

- ◆ Be realistic, but don't be too cautious in planning to challenge the given circumstances!

TIPS ON PLANNING

Agenda

Use the following grid to map out the issues to be negotiated and to prepare for the response you anticipate the employer will have to your position. Refer to the sample entry for help.

ISSUE	YOUR POSITION (INTEREST)	RATIONALE (NEED)	EMPLOYER POSITION (INTEREST)	EMPLOYER RATIONALE (NEED)	YOUR RESPONSE
Relocation	I am very interested in the job, and I think I would do well with this company. However, I need relocation support to make it possible to move within reasonable commuting distance of the new workplace.	I just bought a new home. I have a number of one-time, first-year homeowner expenses to recoup, and selling the house myself would take a lot of work and a long time.	I would like to fill the job immediately and have the new employee begin work as soon as possible to minimize business disruption. This candidate is highly qualified and would be an asset to the company. However, hiring policy exceptions are frowned on here.	We are a highly structured organization and I need to adhere to our established relocation program, which provides minimal relocation assistance for a move of less than 60 miles.	According to my research, most employers in this area offer relocation assistance to seasoned recruits. The time required to sell the house myself doesn't make sense, giving the urgency to bring me on board. Would you consider a signing bonus that would help me manage the cost of selling the house? I would then be free to undertake the search for a new home right away.

ISSUE	YOUR POSITION (INTEREST)	RATIONALE (NEED)	EMPLOYER POSITION (INTEREST)	EMPLOYER RATIONALE (NEED)	YOUR RESPONSE

continues

continued

ISSUE	YOUR POSITION (INTEREST)	RATIONALE (NEED)	EMPLOYER POSITION (INTEREST)	EMPLOYER RATIONALE (NEED)	YOUR RESPONSE

STRATEGY

WHAT IS STRATEGY ALL ABOUT?

Strategy is the art of maximizing your plan's effectiveness by selectively focusing all available resources toward achieving your goal. It is determining *the means* you will use to get to the outcome you desire.

An important part of planning a negotiation is determining the strategy you will use. Ideally, negotiation is guided by a strategy, setting direction for the plan, and a more detailed program of action for achieving the goal and objectives. Negotiation strategies involve *techniques that can be learned.*

HOW DOES STRATEGY AFFECT YOU?

Prepare Mentally

The strategy you develop for a negotiation will reflect your goals and leverage your strengths, while downplaying any weaknesses. Take control of the process by *creating a vision,* or mental picture, of your negotiation strategy, developing supporting points, and brushing up on negotiation skills. By doing these things, you will significantly increase the probability of a successful outcome. Some people find that they can reach the optimal mindset through repeating an affirmation, such as, "I am well prepared for negotiation; I handle negotiations confidently and successfully."

Build your confidence by confirming your situational power sources and impact areas, which you identified in the planning phase. *Power sources* include economics, supply-and-demand considerations, time constraints, precedents and practices, your short- and long-term goals, and the other viable options you have.

Manage the Process

To the extent possible, *establish a safe environment* in which both parties feel comfortable. Soft negotiations are governed by a manner of working together and clearly differentiating between the people (the relationship) and the problem (the issues) involved. People have different points of view and different beliefs about what is really important.

Use a Win-Win Approach

Approach the employer positively, as *an active partner,* rather than defensively. Be prepared to initiate a discussion to set the stage for the negotiation by talking about the negotiation process and customary procedure. Agree on the criteria for evaluating the quality of the discussion.

View the negotiation as a forum for an exchange of ideas. Establish a tone of cooperation and collaboration. Stress common or aligned interests and the potential in your ideas to further organizational goals. Address your value to the employer in terms of your ability relative to the job functions; use your interpersonal skills to establish rapport and reaffirm your commitment to the company and the job. Keep the focus on how you can contribute to the business.

Identify and Address the Issues

Begin the negotiation by complimenting the positive aspects of the job offer on the table. Introduce your preferences as a contextual framework, confirming the points on which you both agree. Sometimes it is wise to start negotiating with a smaller request, to test the waters, and then tackle more difficult issues. But don't waste negotiating power on trivial points.

Negotiation often involves some degree of compromise. By planning, you've determined what you must have—and what you are willing to exchange. You know what your interests are, and you have differentiated between what you need and what you want. Your solution, however, may not be the *only* solution. Rather than take an unyielding position, *furnish alternatives.*

Think from the organization's perspective, and be aware of the disadvantages of high turnover to the employer. Turnover costs can include a former employee's severance payments and benefits continuation, unemployment taxes, and new-hire recruiting and training expenses, as well as the loss of production. It is usually in the employer's interest to do whatever is feasible to attract and *retain* a diverse, highly skilled workforce, building bench strength in sought-after expertise.

Present your case and cast your proposals in the light of common sense and business costs and benefits. Be prepared with a ready rationale to relate your position to employer interests, and have reasonable solutions to anticipated objections. Acknowledge objections and move on; if it is a critical issue, return to the subject in question later in the discussion. Be sure to have your thoughts organized. In the planning phase, think in terms of easy-to-remember "threes"—assemble three points to support each of your positions.

Manage Expectations

You decided your limits in the planning stage, before beginning the actual negotiations. Position yourself to make contingent counter-offers. Counter-offers are an expected part of negotiation. Respond by first reaffirming your interest and qualifications, then pose your suggestion. Stay flexible and *always keep the negotiations open.* Be comfortable with silence and avoid overstating your case.

Stay on Track

Remain focused. Appeals to the common good, image, or others' opinions are not issue-oriented. Have available and refer to independent standards. Evaluate concessions objectively: "How much will this concession cost?" "What can I expect in return?" Know the best alternative. Remember that *concessions should be earned, not volunteered.* Always use "if-then" language. Know when to stand your ground reasonably and when to let go of an issue.

The axiom that "you have to give in order to get" holds true. As part of your strategy, plan what material you can give ahead of time and give only what you can afford. As an example, you might be willing to relinquish something you want—perhaps wished-for extended vacation time—in exchange for the ongoing flexibility you really *need* during the work week to accommodate child-care demands.

Be Realistic

The dynamics of negotiations are often subtle. Watch for negative signals from the other party. Don't allow the negotiation to be jeopardized or to collapse unnecessarily. Presenting a long list of relatively small items risks creating the impression that you may be difficult to work with. A candidate who is inordinately concerned about the company's policies on vacation time, scheduled holidays, and overtime, for example, may be perceived as lacking a commitment to the goals of the business. *Use good judgment* in presenting and pursuing your personal agenda.

FROM THE EMPLOYER'S SIDE OF THE TABLE

Flexibility contributes to a company's ability to retain valued employees. See the negotiation as an opportunity for forging agreement. Review and acknowledge the recruit's potential value to the company. Rather than taking a rigid or negative posture, establish your tolerance for discussion. Encourage the candidate to articulate any questions about the offer. Understand concerns and explore what, if anything, to do about the issues the recruit raises. If there is little room to meet the candidate's needs at this point in time, perhaps an acceptable longer-term solution can be worked out. Should you consider making any significant changes in the "usual" way of doing things, be sure it is with the stipulation that these changes be reviewed and approved as necessary. Don't make any promises that you can't keep!

Although planned turnover of a workforce may at times be a business reality today, the effect of losing and replacing employees under any circumstances is complex. Depending on the business and the position, a number of costs are associated with the departing worker, such as administrative time and any expenditures for severance and unemployment. Extended costs encompass the loss of the worker's knowledge and the effect on other workers who may be required to absorb the terminating employee's work, and in doing so perhaps generating unplanned overtime pay or compensatory time off. Filling a position is also costly in terms of advertising and search charges and recruiting expenses, including applicant travel and accommodations, interviewing, and testing. Once the new employee is on the job, there may be training costs to consider. The learning curve may impact the resumption of production, demanding additional supervisory attention and the time of other workers, and lowering overall productivity. Many organizations make little or no formal effort to evaluate turnover. However, your human resources or accounting support personnel should be able provide guidance in calculating the cost of turnover in your area. Losing and replacing employees represents a considerable— and to a significant extent manageable—bottom-line expense.

POINTS TO REMEMBER

- ◆ Strategy is about what methods you will use to move through the negotiation process.

- ◆ You can study and plan strategic techniques and responses to opposition ahead of time.

- Consider beginning with issues on which agreement is likely, then move on to the more difficult negotiables.

- During negotiation, continually stress mutual benefit, cost consciousness, and added value.

- Win-win negotiating is collaborative in nature.

TIPS ON STRATEGY

Tools for Preparing to Negotiate a Job Offer or Work Agreement

Gather the following while planning negotiations:

- Name, title, location, and telephone number of the party with whom you are negotiating

- Previous correspondence with that person or with the company in general

- Notes and questions

- Organizational information and materials, including an employee handbook

- Self-marketing statement

- Copy of your resume

- Samples of your work for reference, if appropriate

- Professional recommendations

- Business cards

- Pen and notepad

- Proposed process and criteria

- A loosely drafted agenda, prioritized negotiables, and cost-benefit worksheets

- Industry and profession-specific salary and benefit survey information, relocation norms, and cost-of-living data

Negotiation Tactics

Many well known techniques can influence the outcome of negotiations. Some involve packaging—the splitting or combining (bundling) of issues for discussion in an effort to present the matter in the most favorable light. The following table contains positive and negative negotiating techniques that may be used by either side. It's useful to review these techniques so that you can use a particular approach when it would be advantageous (and avoid unscrupulous ones). It's also especially useful in helping you recognize when someone else is using a defined negotiation technique.

MANIPULATIVE	COULD BE MANIPULATIVE OR LEGITIMATE APPROACH	UP-FRONT COMMUNICATION
Deceptive or testing; lessens trust or power-linked intimidation	Evaluate in context	Encouraging trust and win-win agreement
Controlling the agenda or having a hidden agenda	Proposing an agenda	Beginning with a review of aligned interests
Lowballing and "Mother Hubbard" (the cupboard is bare)	Observations about current trends and conditions	Statement of fair dealing
Feinting—bluffing or placing exaggerated importance on a lesser point	Asking for something that incorporates an objective	Redefining the issue; reframing
Imposition of deadlines and time pressures	Withdrawal or (perceived) retreat; waiting the other side out	Reflective silence; deferring decision (breaking to reevaluate)
"Columbo"— "One more thing"— add-ons	The surprise proposal	Using conditional language
Russian Front—forcing a choice between two bad alternatives	Splitting the difference	Tactfully challenging statement

MANIPULATIVE	COULD BE MANIPULATIVE OR LEGITIMATE APPROACH	UP-FRONT COMMUNICATION
Good guy/bad guy (The "Denver System") —claim of limited authority to make the decision	"Salami"—obtaining concessions a little at a time	Pinpointing the business need
Fait Accompli— reference as standard practice and assume it's a done deal before accepting or declining	Bundling or unbundling	Requesting time to consider the terms of the renegotiated offer

CHAPTER 8

Phase II: Negotiating to Agreement

NEGOTIATION VIEWPOINT

Skilled communication is *the key element* in every negotiation proceeding. Remember, negotiation is a two-phase process; the first is grounded in thorough analysis and planning, while the second is founded in communication and draws upon interpersonal skills and active listening.

INTERPERSONAL COMMUNICATION

WHAT IS INTERPERSONAL COMMUNICATION ALL ABOUT?

Interpersonal communication is an ongoing interactive process through which we create meaning, send and receive messages and feedback, and confirm or adjust our understanding of the messages being conveyed.

In putting it all together, how we communicate—framing, advocating, illustrating, and inquiring—creates a lasting impression on others. Research and planning place communications on a sure footing, but solid, persuasive communications skills are required to get the message across effectively. By establishing rapport and a win-win climate of openness up front, the tenor is set for successful negotiations.

HOW DOES INTERPERSONAL COMMUNICATION AFFECT YOU?

Negotiation is an extension of your interviewing skills. You have already managed the screening interview and, perhaps, a second and even a third interview where the objective was to assess whether there was a match to the job. Continue to draw upon your earlier interviewing preparation and experience as you work through the negotiation process.

If both parties are satisfied, each will work to make the agreement and the relationship succeed. Different people have different needs and place different weight or value on things. There are always reasons to negotiate and advantages to be gained by both parties.

FROM THE EMPLOYER'S SIDE OF THE TABLE

As an employer, you have successfully used your interpersonal and diplomatic skills in a variety of ways to achieve your business goals. Make use of these same abilities in the negotiation process. Notes in your negotiations playbook should include founding the negotiation process on the concept of teamwork. First, identify common objectives and determine the criteria for win-win success. Recognize and admit differences candidly. Then transcend any perception of incompatible interests by acknowledging that there are multiple paths to achieving success and reinforcing the overriding goal—a mutually beneficial employment arrangement.

While you may have gleaned some inkling of what a worker's needs are during the interviewing phase, wait until you hear them fully articulated by the prospective employee. Make it easy for the candidate to discuss concerns. Take the individual worker's situation, as well as business circumstances, into account. Try to agree on a statement describing the principal issue(s), and keep the focus on problem resolution. When listening to the recruit, concentrate on what is really being said. Ask questions and paraphrase. Make sure that you understand what lies behind exceptional requests. Try to communicate information in a way that builds and reinforces the relationship at the same time. Determine what would be acceptable for now, and what would be acceptable over time.

POINTS TO REMEMBER

- ◆ Communications skills are a significant advantage in negotiation.

- ◆ Positive phrasing of points and proposals is important.

- ◆ If there appears to be little or no room for negotiation currently, focus on the future.

TIPS ON INTERPERSONAL COMMUNICATION

Approaching the Negotiation

Assess the audience—the person(s) you will be negotiating with—and adopt an appropriate communication style. Organize a main theme and identify key points. Concentrate on how your uniqueness will add value to the business, while contributing to controlling costs. Demonstrate your potential effect on new initiatives and/or productivity. Make the decision ahead of time whether to begin with a minor issue that will be easy to resolve or to present an issue of major importance to you. *Take and present a long-term view.*

The Exploration Stage

Initiate the discussion with a positive statement, then wait for feedback. Frame the negotiation with a general statement of your *mutual goals.* Keep the interaction low-key. In the exploration period, confirm or adjust your perceptions of the employer's needs. Demonstrate that you understand the other party's position, perhaps by using comparison or analogy.

Build trust. Gain agreement on aligned issues. Stress your commitment and credibility, as well as your expertise, competence, and ability to get things done. Maintaining an air of reasonability will positively affect the climate of the negotiation process. In win-win negotiations, the goal is to work together to look for a mutually agreeable outcome. Keep the focus on what *both* parties want.

The Relationship

Valuing the relationship you have established with the employer is paramount. Remember that you will be working with the person with whom you are negotiating. Pushing too hard, taking a hard line or an adversarial posture, or letting the discussion deteriorate into a contest are counterproductive in the long run.

When an issue surfaces, avoid attempts to personalize it. Appreciate that you and the employer have different needs to be met, rather than thinking in win-lose terms. Use tact and diplomacy. Make it your personal creed when engaged in negotiation to "save face" on behalf of the other party.

Language

Persuasion is the ability to change or influence a belief. *Persuade, rather than coerce.* Use inclusive phrases and "if" statements; establish a common ground for agreement; for example, "If we accept that it will be necessary for me to work every other Saturday, would you agree that some additional vacation time might be arranged?" Practice phrasing a compromise opening, such as, "What if" or "How about," or "Would you feel" to the listener. Restate, or *echo*, frequently. Create, and be comfortable with, conversational and reflective silence.

Always try to have the negotiations take place face to face. This is especially valuable in the initial negotiations, when you are establishing trust. Body language is important. Convey goodwill and attentiveness with your facial expressions and a relaxed, open posture. Dress and look the part of your new job.

Conflict

Conflict can be constructive and positive. Some level of conflict is inevitable; disagreement and conflict are a natural part of the negotiation process. The give and take of different points of view serve a purpose, helping determine what is important to each party. Institute a reasonable challenge. Working through conflict clarifies thinking and the needs, not just the wants or interests, of the other party.

Remain objective and focused on your priorities. In most negotiations, patterns can be distinguished relative to the terms of "give and get," such as both giving, giving if getting, and so forth. Remember, *conflict is only disagreement,* and it's a necessary part of the negotiation process. Refusal to meet your requirements is not rejection of you as an individual or as a future employee.

Beware of making evaluative or absolute statements in your negotiations. Describe the benefits of your proposals to the employer. In a stalemate, neither side is willing to move and the negotiation fails. Approach a difficult issue by asking yourself, "How can I resolve this?" "How could the employer resolve this?" What adjustments or conditions would facilitate resolution, and what could be expected in return?

Continue to identify and assess options and possible approaches to settling issues throughout the negotiation process. Remember that nothing is free. A good agreement requires both participants to give and receive concessions; what is to be determined is only how much, and when.

Let's Stay in Touch

When you meet resistance, be persistent, but know when to let go. If negotiations cannot be concluded on the spot, ask the following questions:

- "Are there any reservations, or reasons that my proposals wouldn't be considered?"

- "What are our next steps and what is the timing?"

When you get stuck, *take a break,* make a small concession, or offer to meet halfway. Suggest integrative solutions, which are more likely to facilitate moving forward. *Never* be adversarial, but rather explore possibilities and continue to extend the same flexibility and understanding you are hoping to receive.

Closing

Know when to conclude. And when you do conclude, hold your ground pleasantly. Be patient. Don't press too quickly for closure. Allow some reflective quietude, time to consider what is on the table.

Once a satisfactory agreement is arrived at, summarize it. A written follow-up will underscore the legitimacy of the process and help avoid the possibility of any misunderstanding. An informal review, in writing, of a verbal agreement often works well. Introduce your follow-up by mentioning your pleasure with the process and the relationship, then, "Following is a summary of my understanding of our agreement" or "This is my understanding of what we agreed to." Conclude with a positive statement about the agreement and an expression of your appreciation. Verbal agreements should always be *tactfully* confirmed in writing.

If, after careful consideration, you determine that you and the employer have been unable to reach a mutually satisfactory understanding, be sure to call to let him or her know of your decision. Then send a letter of declination, expressing your appreciation for the offer and keeping the door open for future opportunities to work together.

In some instances, a job candidate may be considering more than one offer simultaneously. In communicating with competing employers, it's usually best to be up-front about the situation, but be sure to avoid any appearance of playing one offer against the other. Once you have made a decision, notify the employer of choice, then the competing employer.

When declining, stress the appeal of the offers and companies and point out that for many reasons, you chose the offer most suited to you personally at this time. Follow up with a thank-you letter, conveying your appreciation of the offer and the time spent with you and suggesting you keep in touch with one another. In this era of business networking and constant change, you might observe (if it fits the occasion) that you could be working together in the future, one way or another!

TIPS ON LANGUAGE
Ask, but don't assume!

Use *what*, not *why*, in framing questions. Conditional language that softens the message when appropriate, such as the following phrases, greatly facilitates negotiations. Never react with a flat "no"; rather, pause, consider thoughtfully, then respond:

"That is not going to work."

Continue reasonably, with an appropriate phrase; for example:

"Are you willing to…?"

"What would you consider?"

"What are the alternatives?"

"I understand your concerns."

"I am able/I can…"

"Do you agree that…?"

"There are some things I would like to discuss."

"I would like to consider/have you considered…?"

"Would you think about…?"

"Oh, by the way…"

"What is reasonable?"

"Generally…"

"What is the opportunity for…?"

"What if/in lieu of…?"

"What is the approval process?"

"I would like your thoughts on…"

"These are my problems."

"Can we talk about…?"

"Can we explore the possibility of…?"

"Is there anything you might be able to do about…?"

"One of the things that is quite common is…"

"There are a few things I am having a problem with…"

"Is there anything/anything else the company can do?"

"At what level do _____ kick in?" (bonuses/benefits/perks)

COMMUNICATIONS MAGIC– ACTIVE LISTENING

WHAT IS ACTIVE LISTENING ALL ABOUT?

One of the most critical interpersonal communications skills is the ability to listen well. With active listening, the listener reflects back (repeats) what he has heard to acknowledge understanding and provide the opportunity for further clarification. Active listening emphasizes sensitivity to the other party's reactions and feelings and the ability to see things from their point of view.

Listening skills encompass frequent restatement of positions through asking clarifying questions, emphasizing points of agreement, and adopting a "team" or "we could" attitude. As the negotiation proceeds, active listening becomes highly contributory to a successful outcome. Communication must be responsive to the situation, to the sometimes unpredictable or unintentional messages that the other party is sending.

HOW DOES ACTIVE LISTENING AFFECT YOU?

Don't assume understanding on your part, or on the part of the other person. Use active listening to reflect your initial understanding of the information conveyed. Checking back by asking questions allows you to assess progress and avoid possible derailment along the route to a successful agreement.

As the negotiation progresses, ask yourself:

> "How are issues and concerns being expressed?" "Are there hidden needs not yet acknowledged that must be brought to the surface?" "Are incompatibilities being defined and addressed?"

FROM THE EMPLOYER'S SIDE OF THE TABLE

College communications and management training courses often introduce active listening as a component of interpersonal communications. Many hiring managers who have experience interviewing recruits and managing staff listen actively without even consciously thinking about it. To ensure full understanding of the concerns being raised and the agreement being discussed, it is as important for a manager to reflect and clarify the messages being received as it is for a candidate to do so.

POINTS TO REMEMBER

- Active listening is a skill; it can be acquired.

- Listening actively will give you clues, additional cues to which you can consciously tailor your response.

- Active listening enhances the negotiation communications significantly and reduces the likelihood of any misunderstandings.

TIPS ON ACTIVE LISTENING

Communications Checklist

PREPARATION

- Research the company.

- Plan presentation relative to the job; prepare examples, positive responses, and thoughtful alternatives.

REHEARSAL

- Practice.

- Speak out loud.

- Use a reasonable tone of voice.

APPEARANCE

- Be well groomed.

- Maintain a professional demeanor.

COMMUNICATION

- Speak in a well-modulated tone.

- Make eye contact.

- Use effective body language.

- Listen actively.

- Relax. Smile!

PACKAGE

- Assemble relevant reference materials.

- Bring samples of work products, if relevant.

CONTRACTS

WHAT ARE CONTRACTS ALL ABOUT?

Employment covenants are protective; they document reciprocal rights and obligations. Contracts of employment are especially useful in situations where a number of employment variables are being negotiated.

With some exceptions, contracts are more a standard practice abroad than they are in the United States, where many companies operate on an "employment at will" basis.

HOW DO CONTRACTS AFFECT YOU?

Ask whether and under what circumstances the company would consider an employment contract. Preferably, have the contract prepared by an attorney. You may be offered the opportunity to summarize the agreement reflecting the conditions of your employment. Take care that all negotiated items are covered in detail in any written document.

You could make your acceptance of the job contingent upon receipt of a written contract. Request and schedule a follow-up meeting to respond to a written offer, if one is presented. If there is no written contract, then introduce the idea of a written summary of any agreement negotiated. Frame it as commonly desirable, a detailing of the terms of the offer that is essential for clarity, review, and discussion. The contract should cover "what-ifs"—if the company opts out, continuances of benefits; if you back out, penalties. Think through and document the circumstances surrounding possible termination "for cause." In troubled economic times or instances of employer financial vulnerability, a contract becomes very important. "Golden parachutes" soften the potential impact of job loss under certain circumstances, providing for advantageous compensation and/or benefits payouts in the event of change of control of the company, usually combined with termination.

Contract Workers

Although it is being strongly challenged by workers, interim and contingent employment has been a growing field with the just-in-time management concept and the trend toward outsourcing. Salaries for such work may be negotiated to pay a premium, to offset reduced or nonexistent benefits coverage. Sometimes, medical benefits can be negotiated, especially in a "temp-to-perm" situation, where a firm uses temporary assignments to look over potential employees before putting them on the full-time regular payroll. Independent contractor assignments can and should be negotiated as well. Here, critical contract elements are much more extensive and include detailed definitions of deliverables, project scope and responsibility roles, timeframes, and resources.

If your job offer is for other than full-time regular employment, in addition to pay, consider suggesting a joint review of the following negotiables:

- ◆ Bonus opportunity

- ◆ Benefits and work-related insurance requirements

- ◆ First bid rights on full-time openings

- ◆ Performance and status reviews for long-term assignments

- ◆ Proprietary information/materials (project work) rights

- ◆ Conflict-of-interest provisions

FROM THE EMPLOYER'S SIDE OF THE TABLE

Feel comfortable with a request for a contract or letter of agreement, which should not indicate a lack of trust on the part of the worker, but rather a desire to ensure full mutual understanding of the terms of employment. Such understanding is in the best interest of both parties.

In the case of any contract arrangement, include quantitative data wherever possible to clarify expectations. Set out performance and work product review and approval conventions, timeframes and project parameters to avoid or discourage future disagreement. An employer may also want to specify a code of conduct regarding ownership of intellectual property, trade secrets, and client bases.

POINTS TO REMEMBER

- ◆ Contracts are very desirable when it is important to thoroughly document rights and obligations.

- ◆ A contract should not indicate lack of trust on the part of either party; rather, it ensures mutual understanding.

THE AGREEMENT—GET IT IN WRITING

Employment contracts should always be reviewed by attorneys for both parties.

ELEMENTS OF AN EMPLOYMENT CONTRACT

- Names of parties and the employing organization
- Job title and organizational reporting structure
- Job functions
- Decision date
- Contract date and signatures
- Start date
- Work location and work schedule
- Terms and timing of compensation agreement, including bonus plans and terms, and first-period bonus guarantee
- Provision for necessary insurances
- Performance measures and review timeframes

BENEFITS, INCLUDING SPECIAL TERMS OF THE AGREEMENT, SUCH AS EARLY BENEFITS VESTING

- Medical/dental
- Income protection and life insurance
- Relocation
- Pension and retirement
- Vacation
- Work and family arrangements
- Business and travel expense reimbursement
- Supplemental benefits
- Perquisites

GENERAL AGREEMENT PROVISIONS INCLUDING PERIODIC REVIEW OF AGREEMENT ARRANGEMENTS

- Termination of employment: death, disability, cause, other than cause

- Procedures to address exceptions post-agreement

- Confidentiality, proprietary clauses

- Disagreement relief, arbitration

CONTINGENCIES AND RESOLUTIONS

- Reference and security checks

- Drug test

PART IV

The Negotiables—Job Design and Compensation

T*his section discusses job design and content, and forms of direct employee compensation: base pay, variable pay, and long-term incentives—some of the monetary and nonmonetary work rewards for which you will be bargaining when you sit down to negotiate an employment package. By knowing your options in matters of job design and compensation, you can determine which specific items in each area are open to negotiation. The included analysis worksheets will enable you to evaluate a compensation offer against the compensation for your current or most recent job, or against a second offer.*

CHAPTER 9

Job Design

NEGOTIATION VIEWPOINT

The matching of a candidate with a job is a joint venture involving both the applicant and the potential employer. Each has interests at stake and wants the relationship to be successful. An early part of the job-offer negotiation is the process of presenting, discussing, and agreeing upon the job objectives and how an individual's skills and abilities will be used in the workplace.

As we move forward in a service- and information-based economy, how we work—how work is structured and the nature of work itself—is changing. Job design and content can be confining, or it can be an opportunity to expand the individual's, and therefore the organization's, capabilities. By looking at the position objectives and the work components, you can determine the "fit" with your strengths and goals. In assessing fit, remember to think about time allocation, including development and the lifelong learning required in the current work environment.

WHAT IS JOB DESIGN ALL ABOUT?

A job is a set of affiliated work functions characterized by required knowledge, skill, effort, responsibility, and the conditions surrounding the work being performed. Stability of job content as a static set of functions is rapidly becoming an obsolete concept, replaced with the view that work is constantly being reshaped by technology and new products. The job is evolving into a broader set of responsibilities and becoming a workstation, a project, or an assignment. A position is one job, sometimes forged by the person doing the work.

The rules are being rewritten and work is being viewed and performed differently. Work functions—what we will be doing in the organization, and how—are no longer set in stone. The design of a job may be negotiable. Rapidly changing jobs create a need for ongoing learning. With this fundamental change comes an opportunity to enhance your job satisfaction by reexamining job design.

Job satisfaction is affected by a combination of variety, completion or closure, significance or connection, independence, and interaction. People find their work to be meaningful when it enables them to use a range of skills, to learn, to see, and to be responsible for a finished work product, and to identify with the nature of the work itself and the role of their work in the business. The degree of independence in a job, work relationships, and the chance to contribute and receive feedback on work results all play a part in job satisfaction. Recognition and acknowledgement of a job well done also contribute to satisfaction with work.

Because jobs and positions are generally composed of several work functions, it is often possible to combine and recombine these functions and supporting tasks to create a position tailored to an individual's strengths and interests, while still meeting the needs of the organization. However, management sometimes resists the introduction of employee discretion, which would allow employees more control over job design, job content, and how to accomplish the work. Specific uneasiness with greater worker autonomy is fueled by concerns about reduced management authority, employees "taking advantage," and the increased difficulty of supervising, managing, and evaluating worker performance.

HOW DOES JOB DESIGN AFFECT YOU?

Clarify the position, obtaining as much information about the job as possible. Craft an acceptable position description if one is not available. When providing input to the design and documentation of a job, keep in mind that job descriptions should summarize the most important functions of a job and not become a long list of tasks performed in support of job functions. Nail down the design and content of the job before you accept the offer by asking the right questions.

Here's where your research will be helpful. Review your work strengths and weaknesses, likes and dislikes. Then look at the organizational culture, vision, and values. Is it structured or open? Formal or casual? If you haven't already done so, ask for a tour of the facility and the department where you will be working. What is the management style? How is performance measured and evaluated? Consider the risk and reward/recognition opportunity.

Take into account the business environment. Where is the organization in its business life cycle? What is its future direction? Align your job design and job content proposals with the company's direction and strategic planning. Know the company's business model and financial picture. What is the specific added value of the position in supporting employer goals? What is the unique added value that you bring to the position?

FROM THE EMPLOYER'S SIDE OF THE TABLE

Job content and the sense of performing meaningful work are often what attract a worker to a choice of occupation and even to a particular employer and job opportunity. In addition to compensation, the chance to work within the individual's area of interest, the desire to make a contribution, the need for learning and growth, and the wish to build quality work relationships are important to people today.

It is advantageous for the employee to have an understanding of the general work flow within which his or her job operates and how the work performed contributes to the goals of the organization. The hiring manager should make every effort to help the potential employee understand his or her prospective role in meeting the organization's business objectives. Most companies maintain job descriptions in some form; however, with an eye to the larger context in which work is performed, employers are getting away from documenting job content too narrowly or specifically. Overly detailed work descriptions are administratively cumbersome documents, and the pace of organizational change necessitates constant rewriting and reevaluation. It is often more efficient to work with broad, functional descriptions, focusing on the job accountabilities and responsibilities and the principal duties of the job. Greater detail, if desired, can be recorded in an employee's performance plan, which must by its nature be revisited periodically.

It is usually in the mutual interest of the employer and the employee to create an environment that encourages development through creative job design and work flexibility. When defining a job, consider the big picture. Build in the opportunity for workers to receive cross-training in other related areas. Employees will appreciate the chance to expand their skills, and over time, you will develop an adaptable workforce. Enhancing the employee knowledge base allows the organization to provide better coverage and redeploy workers at little or no additional cost.

POINTS TO REMEMBER

- How we work—how work is structured and the nature of work itself— is changing.

- It's important to both the employer and the employee that the job be a good "fit."

- The design of a job may be negotiable.

- Understand the job and what you will contribute to it—as well as how the position will be of benefit you.

POSITION DEFINITION/JOB-FIT ANALYSIS

Does the open position make the most of your strengths and give you the opportunity to continue your career growth? Review your resume and identify specific areas of job design, job content, and control over work that you want to address during negotiations.

CONTEXT

Industry trends and growth prospects

ORGANIZATIONAL STRUCTURE

Senior management/company goals

Partnerships and alliances

Markets/new markets and products/new products

Management style/tolerance for innovation

Organizational reporting/matrixed relationships

Work flow

Span of control

Scope of authority and discretion, and decision-making responsibilities

JOB ACCOUNTABILITIES/OBJECTIVES/DELIVERABLES

Short-term and long-term department goals

Client/customer base

Job functions

Immediate problems/priorities and most important contribution

RESOURCES

Information distribution/communication loops

People (staff), number and qualifications, administrative support

Technology

Budget

Time

RISK AND REWARD

Performance appraisal system, measures, review timetable and standards

Rewards/recognition

DEVELOPMENT

Career path flexibility/progression

Professional growth

ACCOUTREMENTS

Title

Status

Perks

CHAPTER 10

Compensation

NEGOTIATION VIEWPOINT

Carefully exploring all of the employment options and tangible and intangible rewards of the job offer in the transition from candidate to new employee is an exciting prospect. It puts you in the best possible situation to ensure that your successful job search is also the beginning of a successful new phase of your career. Employment packages are the exchange structure between the company and the employee.

WHAT IS COMPENSATION ALL ABOUT?

Total compensation is a combination of base pay, variable pay, and benefits. It is an appropriately equivalent payment, counterbalancing an exchange for the work performed. An organization's compensation strategy is founded in competitive positioning and can be influenced by industry norms. Cash compensation—base and variable pay—is structured by a company's pay program and guidelines for base pay and any additional variable compensation for which an employee is eligible.

Compensation philosophy and programs are impacted by external factors that include the business, economic, governmental, and regulatory climate, as well as by the company's organizational culture and business strategy internally. Long-term business plans affect employer programs. The bigger picture from the company standpoint encompasses overall business goals and the human resource consequences of business objectives—for instance, the stability of the workforce and the skills the company needs now and in the future.

A company's place in the business life cycle—startup, growth, maturity, or renewal—and the nature of the work performed influence its pay philosophy, how it positions pay relative to the market (and the definition of that market), and the base salary, variable pay, and cash/noncash mix. Salaries are frequently an organization's largest budgeted expense. Often, many other employee benefits are related directly to base salary level; for example, formulas for levels of life insurance coverage, short-term and long-term disability pay, defined-benefit pension, and 401(k) employer contributions may be pegged to a percent of base salary.

Today, we think in terms of total compensation. Total compensation is the sum of base salary, bonus, and long-term incentive and the value of benefits. Equitable total compensation is thought to be equivalent to the value of the service given and the results achieved.

HOW DOES COMPENSATION AFFECT YOU?

Organizations accomplish their objectives through people. Investments in employees include both monetary and nonmonetary compensation. People are motivated by different combinations and various forms of total compensation. Today, employers have begun to design competitive, employee-responsive programs through the innovative use of rewards. There is an implicit interdependence between employees' knowledge, skills, and abilities, and their salary and benefits. Factors in determining compensation include the competitive market pay, affordability, internal relativity, and relocation and other new-hire expenses, such as training. The value of benefits is also taken into account. Employers are making greater efforts to communicate the dollar worth of their benefits programs, which run the gamut from minimal, legislatively required benefits to very rich, full-spectrum packages. Independent contractors and others working under alternative work arrangements need to consider all of the components of total compensation in pricing their services.

Compensation programs are a bridge between reward theory and motivation, between the employer and the employee. Rewards are categorized as extrinsic and intrinsic. Extrinsic rewards are those that a person receives from sources other than the work itself, such as compensation, benefits, development, promotions, vacations, and other outcomes apart from the job. Intrinsic rewards are associated specifically with the position itself, and stem from how a person perceives and relates to the job and the work being performed.

You don't need to become an expert in compensation and benefits to negotiate a job offer; you simply need to get acquainted with what the questions are. To evaluate a compensation package, ask yourself how each component affects you. What is the relevance of each of the elements in the package? What is the implication of the whole package in relationship to who you are and what you want to accomplish?

Will the offered position reward you in proportion to your expected contribution? Will you have the opportunity to advance professionally and increase your compensation through periodic reassessment of your base salary and bonus opportunity? How will performance be factored into the picture? Consider the value of the total compensation package that the employer is offering. The prospect of a 10 percent increase in total compensation usually indicates that a job change is worthwhile.

FROM THE EMPLOYER'S SIDE OF THE TABLE

The animating idea of compensation is to reward current employees who are meeting their objectives and to attract and recruit new employees with the skills the business needs to grow and thrive. While people don't work solely for the paycheck, compensation programs that are properly designed, communicated, and administered act to motivate the behaviors and performance needed to achieve organizational objectives.

It is in the best interest of the organization for rewards to drive business performance through employee performance; therefore, the rewards offered must be the right rewards, at the right time, given to the right people.

Both employers and workers should reassess the individual's compensation package periodically throughout the employment relationship. Most often, the manager, independently or collaboratively with the employee, identifies the individual's work and development objectives and performance expectations, and the employee is responsible for producing the desired performance and results in order to earn a pay increase or benefit. The company's pay program, external competitive pay, internal relativity, and affordability are factored into most pay adjustment decisions.

What is the organization willing to pay for? Hiring managers need to be familiar with the company's compensation philosophy and strategy, which support the business culture and direction. The first step is to look at the business mission; the business plan; and the distinctive knowledge, skills, and abilities of workers needed to achieve the plan objectives. The design of the pay structure then follows logically from such analysis. In an organization with pay ranges for its jobs, an employee's progress through a pay grade may be well defined—for example, time in grade—or flexibly administered, with pay for performance being the mantra. There may be exceptional pay guidelines for workers with skills in high demand. Some disciplines such as engineering or accounting may reference a maturity curve, with pay scales, often market-based, that increase according to time in the profession.

As the organization and its environment change, the skills being rewarded and performance being motivated by a program may no longer be those that are most advantageous for business success. When a company positions pay with an emphasis on competitive market conditions, that strategy can sometimes lead to internal pay inconsistencies. The organization may already have employees who are doing the same work with similar results, but who didn't benefit from the same market conditions at the time they assumed their job duties. On the other hand, pay based solely on internal practices can quickly become out of sync with the external job market and competitive pay. Monitoring and evaluation of pay programs should be ongoing.

Various mixes of cash and equity compensation are the most affordable and effective way to pay at different points in the business life cycle. In very general terms, the following table shows typical compensation vehicles according to a company's position in the business cycle:

PLACE IN BUSINESS LIFE CYCLE	COMPENSATION EMPHASIS
Startup company with limited cash	Equity
Growth company	Short-term and long-term incentives
Mature company with more available cash	Base salary and short-term incentives
Company in decline	Base salary, lump-sum merit increases and benefits
Company in turnaround mode	Short-term incentives

POINTS TO REMEMBER

* You should consider a job's risk and reward/recognition opportunity in negotiations.

* Understanding the employer's perspective is useful when negotiating the compensation and benefits package.

* Total compensation includes salary and variable pay opportunity, benefits, and perquisites.

* Work rewards are both extrinsic and intrinsic.

* Know what the package means in relation to who you are and what you want to accomplish.

* Compensation should be periodically reassessed and readjusted as necessary.

BASE SALARY COMPENSATION

Cash compensation is made up of both base salary and variable pay. Base salary is compensation communicated as an annual, monthly, biweekly, or weekly dollar amount, usually fixed for a period of time. Hourly base pay is the rate of pay per hour for the job being performed.

WHAT IS BASE SALARY COMPENSATION ALL ABOUT?

Pay structure reflects the company's culture and may be modeled on some combination or variation of the following:

- Single fixed rate

- Step rate (based on time in the job or grade)

- Merit range

- Step rate plus merit pay

- Length of time in the job and relationship to the market plus merit pay

- Skill- or competency-based pay

Many companies today continue to use the concepts of merit increases or pay for performance. Others are introducing skill-based pay systems to encourage worker development. Employees with broad skills can be more easily reassigned as business needs and priorities change. Certification requirements to demonstrate skill acquisition are usually defined. Programs may require that knowledge and skill acquisition be preplanned and approved before they are rewarded. Some companies require that the employee demonstrate and apply the knowledge or skills acquired on the job before the employee is granted a pay raise. Competency-based pay rewards employees for progressing through a combination of abilities and technical competence and recognizes both breadth and depth of knowledge.

A base salary range usually identifies the parameters within which salaries are positioned. It represents what the company is willing to pay for the job functions. A salary range may be determined by an internal formula or by the cost of labor—competitive pay for similar or benchmark jobs in the external marketplace—or by a combination thereof. Many companies participate in compensation surveys and refer to survey results to assess competitive pay. Benchmark jobs, used for comparison, are sets of defined work functions that are readily recognizable in or across industries.

A salary range may or may not be adjusted to reflect changes in cost-of-living or labor indices. Some national employers do adjust base salary ranges to acclimate pay to cost-of-living or cost-of-labor differences at their locations in various parts of the country. Quite often, the midpoint between the top and the bottom of the range is reflective of market average or competitive pay:

Salary Range Structure

LOW	MIDPOINT	HIGH
$30,000	$50,000	$70,000

In an organization with a salary range structure, the salary you are offered is arrived at by reviewing the position's salary range; your individual experience, knowledge, and skills; and usually, the market price—how much people are making in similar jobs in other companies, as well as the salaries of current employees doing similar work. Typically, employee pay is clustered around the midpoint, with newly hired, inexperienced employees paid lower in the range and those with significant experience or premium skills paid higher in the range.

In some organizations, the base salary range is viewed as a guideline, not intended to stipulate a single, inflexible dollar amount. Increasingly, companies are referencing competitive data to set pay for core job functions, around which salaries are positioned based on the experience, knowledge, skills, and abilities of the individual and the complexity and multiplicity of the job functions.

Many factors can affect the amount of the base salary and how it is paid to the employee. Shift differential, per diem, and on-call/special schedule adjustments may be made to the base salary. If the job requires that a worker be on call (accessible during some period of time when he or she is not scheduled for work), there may be a premium or formula for additional pay for when the employee is called in to work.

Some companies pay employees a "retainer" or stipend, or allow them to draw a loan against their anticipated commission. Those working overseas are typically granted an expatriate allowance premium and may be eligible for special tax considerations.

Overtime pay is highly regulated by the Fair Labor Standards Act (FLSA). If a job is nonexempt (eligible for overtime pay), it is governed by very specific rules for compensation. There are special exceptions to FLSA requirements for government workers.

HOW DOES BASE SALARY COMPENSATION AFFECT YOU?

When beginning salary discussions with your potential employer, never reveal your salary requirements too soon. The employer may have a higher figure in mind, but if the salary you name is lower, that's what you'll be stuck with. An employer with a lower figure in mind might rule out your candidacy prematurely, considering you "unaffordable" or too demanding.

Instead, be prepared to respond to a preliminary inquiry with a range estimate and ask for more information about all aspects of the job's compensation.

In most pay structures, jobs are assigned to a hierarchical level that reflects relative value and is associated with a salary range. Where a worker's salary falls within the range is influenced by his or her knowledge, skills, abilities, education, experience, and sometimes, grade/time in the job. Employees should have a pragmatic idea of what they need to earn and a clear understanding of what they will need to do to increase their base pay.

In assessing the base salary offer, first determine the company's overall pay philosophy. Know the company's total compensation approach and the level of labor competition it faces. How a business pays its workers often reflects its position in the business life cycle; for example, a well established company may be able to offer more cash compensation, while a startup business may emphasize equity opportunity. Factors that companies consider in determining salary budgets include the business plan, past financial results and future prospects, staffing strategy—the caliber of workers it wants to attract and retain—and affordability—what the employer can afford to pay.

Have a sense of the market and what competitive pay is for similar work. Research pay for similar jobs. You can find published salary surveys in the library or on the Internet, but be sure to consider the reliability of the survey source. Surveys and polls are shaped by the sponsor, the design, the position descriptions, the company participant group, the integrity of the position matching, and the statistical methodology that is applied to produce the survey results. Don't use the job title as a benchmark. The key is how closely the offered position matches the surveyed job functionally and in size and scope of responsibility. The Bureau of Labor Statistics (BLS) surveys are one readily available source of market data. Industry and occupational surveys generally contain data that pertain more closely to specialized work environments and jobs.

Employment firms and employment specialists may be of help in judging market demand and whether certain skills could be worth a premium. Business and trade publications, newspaper employment ads and articles, and people you know in the industry are all potential sources of information. Evaluate the available information realistically. Survey data is *a piece of information* to be considered in making pay decisions; it is not a panacea.

Base salary is often the primary focus of an applicant, but it is not the only factor in considering compensation. In addition to salary, a hiring bonus, sometimes arrived at via a formula such as a percent of base salary, may be placed on the table. If the initial base-salary offer seems low, explore the possibility of a sign-on bonus!

Eligibility for variable-pay programs or annual cash bonuses and the funding, opportunity, and award formulas will also play an important part in evaluating the base pay portion of total compensation. Find out what criteria determine whether you will receive an annual bonus, and how the amount is arrived at.

In addition to bonus opportunity, determine prescribed review intervals. How often is salary reviewed for increase? A six-month, rather than an annual or 18-month, review cycle can provide exponentially greater possibility for future base salary increases. Some companies even allow employees to take a base salary increase as a lump-sum advance, awarding a periodic increase amount as a loan up front, which the employee repays through deduction at a relatively low interest rate over the year.

In some instances, for example where an employee's salary is relatively high when compared to the market or peer employees, he or she may receive a lump-sum merit increase. Such a lump-sum increase does not raise base pay permanently, but rather, is re-earned annually through sustained performance. This is not a bonus program, but it works to avoid unchecked salary escalation, helping the company to manage its fixed salary expense.

Understand the job and the reporting relationships. Inquire discreetly about internal relativities—peer job compensation opportunity—and the average range of compensation for individuals at the same level. To some extent, the existing job was shaped by the person who performed it before you. Recognize the value that your knowledge, skills, and abilities will contribute—will you be able to offer as much or more than the previous employee? On the other hand, acknowledge that a career change, a location change, or an opportunity for learning may be worth more to you than a high salary figure.

Your bargaining power is greatest prior to accepting an offer. So don't settle for a lower base salary than you need and then hope to find ways to improve it later. Negotiate up front for the salary you want and need. Other benefits, such as disability payments and life insurance amounts, can be driven by the base salary level, so it "pays" to make the best deal you can.

FROM THE EMPLOYER'S SIDE OF THE TABLE

The purpose of pay is to attract, retain, motivate and reward workers. Compensation is a tool to enable the achievement of business objectives. At the same time, it is a major cost of doing business.

Funding for base pay is impacted by business conditions and results. In considering a base pay offer, keep in mind the company's pay philosophy and your budget. Factor in the candidate's relevant education and experience, knowledge, skills and abilities, and total compensation opportunity. Be cognizant of what the competition is paying for similar jobs. Ideally, pay is commensurate with the market and individual qualifications and performance.

Pay is governed by a number of laws today. One, the Fair Labor Standards Act (FLSA), sets the minimum wage and standards for exemption from mandatory overtime pay. In the future, revisions to the FLSA may ease overtime calculation requirements and perhaps allow for compensatory time off in lieu of overtime pay for nonexempt work. If a job carries exempt status, it will not receive measured hourly overtime, although some opportunity for project bonus or nonformulaic compensatory time off may exist. In some locations, overriding state regulations are even more stringent than federal edicts. We can expect that economic realities and legislative initiatives will continue to mandate modifications in current pay practices.

In gathering competitive pay information, be aware that antitrust concerns severely restrict employers from sharing compensation data directly between competitors without a third-party screen. In evaluating market data for jobs, look carefully at a survey's participant group, the industries represented, the size of organizations involved, and the geographic locations of the companies and jobs. Analyze the information carefully and focus on the total compensation reflected in the survey. One really germane, valid survey is often more valuable and credible than a number of less relevant sources.

When the base pay offered is not particularly attractive to the candidate, a sign-on bonus may help sway him or her. It is a one-time payment that holds down fixed costs and makes up for some of the advantages of the recruit's current or former position that will be lost in the transition to the new job. For example, the employee may have to leave behind stock options that are not yet exercisable. A sign-on bonus may mitigate the damage and ease the transition. It may also help the recruit's family better accept the changes and the risks associated with a new job.

POINTS TO REMEMBER

- Don't reveal your salary requirements too early in the negotiation process.

- Knowing the pay philosophy of the company, as well as pay levels for similar jobs inside and outside the industry, will help you evaluate a base salary offer.

+ A number of variables—including employee knowledge, skill, and experience; the total compensation opportunity; and future compensation prospects—may impact base salary.

+ In most companies, base salary is the foundation of compensation; determine the opportunities for base salary increase that the company offers.

VARIABLE PAY–SHORT-TERM INCENTIVES AND BONUS PROGRAMS

The trend today is toward more conservative base salaries and higher incentive compensation. More and more employers are moving toward "pay at risk" plans, in which an employee re-earns a portion of his or her pay annually or periodically based upon achieving objectives or exceeding standards. The benefit to the employer is a shift away from fixed cost; the benefit to the employee is more direct influence over the amount of pay he or she earns. The weighting of base salary and variable pay reflects the organization's cultural goals and current mores and the employer's specific business and human resources objectives.

WHAT IS VARIABLE PAY ALL ABOUT?

Variable pay is compensation, either cash or stock (equity) that is tied closely to the performance of the company, a group, or an individual employee. It is a one-time payment that is not added to base pay and varies according to performance results. Variable pay is generally contingent upon the accomplishment of a predetermined goal or objective.

Stock ownership linked to performance is often keyed to responsibility levels—employees with more responsibility for the bottom line receive proportionately more ownership share opportunity. Variable-pay programs must clearly define eligibility, payout formula and frequency, and performance measurements. In some instances, plans may carry a combination of weighted corporate, group, and individual performance components.

Organization-Wide and Group Plans

Profit-sharing plans emphasize overall company performance and generally are based on financial results—for example, net profits or return on equity. Because it is difficult to assume that all employees influence company profits equally, the percentage opportunity may be proportionate to an employee's ability to affect bottom-line results. Profit-sharing plans may be either short-term or long-term, based on the timing of distributions. If all or a portion of the profit-share funds are held inaccessible in a vested account, the long-term deferred return is sometimes structured in the form of a pension plan.

Gainsharing plans measure the value of productivity and allocate shares between the employer and employees. Such plans are usually formula-based, measuring increases in productivity and profitability through cost containment and quality enhancement measured against an established baseline. Gainsharing encourages teamwork and employee commitment by making employees' monetary gains dependent on their own impact on the company's performance.

Large- or small-group financial incentives are often flat dollar amounts divided equally among group members upon successful performance and achievement of goals, such as improvement in operating results or improved performance against a target. Alternatively, a percentage of salary can determine the payout figure. Incentives may be tied to either department or workgroup results and are usually determined by the degree to which the work functions involved influence overall results. Team-based rewards recognize the interdependency of related tasks and the amount of interaction required in accomplishing the team objective.

Individual Short-Term Incentives

Individual incentive programs are organized to encourage high performance and include commission pay systems. Annual bonus plans are the most common. They are usually linked to either a percent of base salary or a formula, such as a percent of the job's salary range midpoint.

Behavioral incentive bonuses are usually a one-time flat dollar amount. They include front-end sign-on bonuses, suggestion awards, service awards, leadership awards, technical achievement awards, project milestones, and early retirement incentives.

Spontaneous "spot" (small cash or symbolic) awards for individuals or teams often involve nominations by supervisors or peers for outstanding contributions after the fact and also differ from an annual bonus because they are awarded and paid out immediately following performance, rather than yearly.

Sometimes workers are presented with special gifts, such as an employment anniversary or a national or local holiday remembrance, as an affirmative gesture. Other forms of recognition include individual publicity in company announcements, awards, and professional recognition at conferences and seminars. Noncash recognition programs, such as gift or dinner certificates, plaques, special perks, and so forth, also acknowledge employee contributions.

Travel and vacation incentives are popular, particularly in sales environments. A company may provide a stay in its condominium, or vouchers for airline travel, hotels, and restaurants to recognize worker achievements. Sometimes the type of trip, destination, length of stay, stipend, and inclusion of a spouse are a negotiable part of the bonus opportunity package.

Key-contributor programs generally have limited eligibility based on job level and/or function, and they are aimed at having a significant impact on profitability, productivity, or competitive advantage. These programs are designed to reward achievement of specific, highly desirable goals and to retain high-potential employees. Well-defined and skillfully administered key-contributor plans can foster a healthy competition among employees.

Some jobs are semi-entrepreneurial; that is, you work for yourself while working for a company, most often in a sales capacity. The employer might support the arrangement by sharing the cost of business equipment, providing business supplies, and lending marketing support. Earnings from sales may or may not be limited or capped.

HOW DOES VARIABLE PAY AFFECT YOU?

Variable pay opportunity allows you to more directly affect your total earnings through your performance. In assessing a job offer, it's important to have a clear understanding of the company's variable-pay programs, plan eligibility, bonus opportunity, and performance criteria.

Most often, management is rewarded on profitability and/or expense control at the level of department and company results, whereas team members—the technical and nontechnical population—are rewarded on production at the level of team and individual results. Because it is difficult to make a significant impact on a company's performance in the first few months of employment, it is common to ask for a guaranteed first-year annual bonus at target performance when negotiating a job offer.

Plan administration can vary, even within one company, regarding tax gross-up of payouts (adding the employee's variable pay award tax liability on top of the award amount). Alternatively, would it be advantageous, in your tax situation, to defer some or all of a bonus, and if so, could this be arranged? Be sure to find out whether variable-pay awards are considered part of eligible compensation when salary- or compensation-dependent benefits are calculated.

FROM THE EMPLOYER'S SIDE OF THE TABLE

Variable pay is one of the most visible and effective means of paying for performance. It is appealing to the employer because it shifts costs from fixed to floating, dependent on achievement of business priorities, goals, and objectives. Steps in establishing a variable-pay plan include identifying business goals; defining participant eligibility; determining the funding mechanism; establishing the rewards vehicles and levels; and setting performance goals and time horizons.

All variable-pay initiatives should be reviewed by the company's accounting, tax, and legal resources. While they represent an expense to the company, plans that meet certain regulatory requirements may qualify for advantageous tax treatment. Variable-pay plans typically must conform to a number of legal and tax compliance tests and accounting standards.

Variable-pay plans allow for a closer relationship between employee performance and business results by linking worker objectives to business goals and rewarding the results. Well-designed programs influence and motivate the desired employee behavior. These programs shine the spotlight on total compensation. When such programs are extended down through the ranks, they drive a strong performance focus throughout the organization.

Stock plans most closely align the interests of the employee, employer, and shareholder. Broad-based stock option plans create an ownership culture, strengthening worker ties with fellow employees and emphasizing organizational and shareholder goals.

Fair and objective measurement criteria and excellent communication are critical to achieving employee buy-in to variable-pay programs. Successful administration of variable pay requires clarity about how an employee's performance will be measured, including a definition of how qualitative (nonquantitative) criteria, such as "people skills," will be evaluated. For variable pay to achieve its objectives, managers must feel comfortable giving awards of different amounts depending on each person's performance.

Highly visible noncash awards such as cars or travel and vacation rewards are valued in some business environs because they highlight desired performance and increase employee morale and loyalty. They may be especially appreciated when they represent a luxury the employees would never have allowed themselves to purchase with an equivalent cash bonus. They are also a public statement of the individual's value to the organization, unlike cash bonuses, which are essentially a private transaction. Employee recognition through nonmonetary results, behavioral awards, and spot awards needs to be carefully managed according to individual and cultural preferences.

POINTS TO REMEMBER

- Placing some portion of compensation in variable-pay and pay-at-risk plans is becoming the norm in many industries.

- Know the company's variable-pay opportunity and reward levels.

- Consider short-term incentives and variable-pay opportunities when evaluating the total compensation package.

- Employee noncash recognition programs acknowledge and encourage individual contributions.

LONG-TERM INCENTIVES

WHAT ARE LONG-TERM INCENTIVES ALL ABOUT?

Long-term incentives, which generally have a plan term of more than one year, take the form of both capital (cash) plans and equity (stock ownership) programs. These programs are intended to link employee gain to that of the company. Long-term cash incentives include various performance unit plans.

Incentives may be "a piece of the pie" in the form of stock ownership or company products. Programs include incentive stock options, certain stock grant and stock purchase plans (and loans to purchase stock), and a variety of sophisticated stock vehicles. Long-term incentives are discussed in more detail in the section on executive compensation in chapter 12, "Additional Employee Benefits," although they are not limited to the executive population.

Stock option programs have eligibility, funding, and opportunity formulas and timeframes for taking advantage of the right to purchase stock. They may offer a deferral vehicle or more time to cash in options following termination or retirement. Employee stock and stock option plans are being pushed further down into or even throughout some organizations, often as a percent of pay. Usually, these programs offer the right to purchase a specific number of shares at a specific price within a certain time period. Some jobs may be more highly leveraged than others; that is, a greater relative weight is placed on variable pay in proportion to salary. In some companies, participation in variable-pay programs may be required of portions of the population.

Another piece of the pie, company product discounts and qualified employee programs are forms of *noncash* (of value, but not readily converted to cash) incentives. Company products are those products, programs, and services that are normally provided to the customer. These are made available to employees at no significant additional cost to the amount that the products cost the company to produce.

HOW DO LONG-TERM INCENTIVES AFFECT YOU?

When negotiating total compensation, stock options and stock ownership offer great opportunity for bridging the difference between cash compensation and desired total compensation. Often, an employer who is unwilling or unable to meet a candidate's salary expectations will be open to a discussion of incorporating stock arrangements as part of the employment offer.

Understand the program basis, timing, vesting (the right to the benefit accrued or some portion thereof) eligibility, and measurement criteria and opportunity. Long-term financial incentives work for both the employer and employee, creating a mutual interest in the company's long-term financial success.

FROM THE EMPLOYER'S SIDE OF THE TABLE

Long-term incentive programs promote the business strategy and future direction of the organization. They are often most appropriate for the senior management of an organization, acting to both reward and retain these key players.

Information about both short- and long-term incentive compensation plans abounds. It can be readily found in business and industry publications. You can also obtain incentive program resources—both materials and services—from management and human resource professional organizations and from consulting firms. Companies that already have incentive plans in place are often willing to share their insights and experiences in implementing and administering variable compensation.

Coordination between short- and long-term incentive programs is important, so that the annual plans do not in any way reward short-term behaviors or performance expediencies that conflict with long-term performance goals and are not in the interest of the company's longer-term strategic direction. The hiring manager should always think about the reward system from the employee's perspective, to ensure that it encourages the desired behavior.

POINTS TO REMEMBER

- Long-term incentives include both cash and equity forms of compensation.

- Stock ownership ties employee interests to those of the employer and shareholders.

- Equity incentives are a way to make up for the difference between a cash compensation offer and desired total compensation.

- Company products, programs, and services may be offered to employees at cost as an incentive.

BASE SALARY AND INCENTIVE WORKSHEET

Use the following worksheet to think through the total compensation makeup of the job offer. For variable-pay opportunity, consider eligibility and vesting rules, funding, award formulas, performance criteria and measurements, payment schedules, and in the case of stock incentives, exercise rights and restrictions.

PLAN FEATURE	WORKER RELATIVE POWER	EMPLOYER FLEXIBILITY	NOTES
Base salary			
Review cycle			
Equity ownership/ stock options			

continues

continued

PLAN FEATURE	WORKER RELATIVE POWER	EMPLOYER FLEXIBILITY	NOTES
Short-term cash incentive			
Long-term incentives			

PART V

More Negotiables— Employee Benefits

This section continues discussion of the items that are up for negotiation in a job offer. It focuses on employee benefits—the basics as well as the "nice to haves."

Basic benefits discussed in this section include health-care insurance, income protection and replacement (for example, disability insurance and life insurance), and retirement and termination provisions. Other less common benefits discussed include flexible work schedules, education programs, dependent care, financial and legal assistance, travel and entertainment reimbursement, relocation assistance, and various executive and supplemental benefits.

CHAPTER 11

Primary Employee Benefits

NEGOTIATION VIEWPOINT

Most employers provide workers with a number of benefits in addition to salary and wages. Once fairly standardized, programs are evolving in reaction to increased government regulation and escalating cost, and adapting in response to worker diversity. The conditions as well as the compensation of work have become more important than ever before to the workers of today. Perception of the value of a reward, the basis for motivation, varies according to an individual's lifestyle and values.

The breadth and depth of options offered vary by company. Many companies can make different arrangements to meet different needs; a menu of benefits allows you to choose and therefore more closely attend to your unique needs. Such flexibility can make mid-career moves easier. The rewards a job carries are both intrinsic and extrinsic. Intrinsic rewards come from job satisfaction—how we feel about the work we do. Extrinsic rewards come in both financial and nonfinancial forms. Total compensation is broken out into direct (cash and equity) compensation and indirect compensation: employee benefits. Common employee benefits include health insurance, income protection, and retirement funding. Indirect benefits also encompass Social Security; unemployment benefits; and workers' compensation, which provides for on-the-job injury medical expenses.

WHAT ARE PRIMARY EMPLOYEE BENEFITS ALL ABOUT?

Employers strive to balance the costs of benefits with the positive results they produce: employee attraction and retention, increased employee motivation, and a reasonable sense of security for employees. These factors combine to enhance the company's image as an employer of choice.

Primary employee benefits include health-care plans, short- and long-term disability coverages, income protection and replacement insurance, death benefits, and retirement and termination payments.

With flexible benefits or cafeteria plans, the employee receives a flex credit—either a uniform fixed dollar amount or an amount determined by salary, length of service, family status, or some other criteria. The employee uses the credit to offset a portion of the cost of the benefits and coverage levels he or she chooses. Often, the company will require the employee to elect a minimum level of coverage; the plan usually addresses employer policy, if any, regarding unused flex credits.

As a rule of thumb, once you have signed up for coverage for elective benefits for the prescribed period, you cannot change your elections until the next open enrollment period, which generally occurs annually. The exception is when you experience a "qualifying event," such as having a child or changing your marital status.

HOW DO PRIMARY EMPLOYEE BENEFITS AFFECT YOU?

Personal philosophy and needs lead to prioritization of benefits. Cafeteria or "menu" plans open the door for negotiation by giving the employer greater latitude in framing the conditions and climate of a job offer and presenting the employee with options and choices based on individual needs and lifestyle preferences.

In general, people continue to be most attentive to matters of health care, retirement, home, education, and personal debt. Workers are sometimes inclined to think in terms of "events" when it comes to benefits—what is urgent and time-sensitive, what is critical for now—rather than concentrating on the importance of long-term planning. However, you should evaluate both short- and long-term needs and goals when selecting the most desirable compensation and benefits package.

Benefits are resources. Which of them do you value? What will bring you the greatest possible return? Shop around and see what benefits you could obtain independently. Compare those costs and coverage levels with what the company is offering. Use this information to set realistic bargaining and leverage points and develop a strategy. Use the worksheet in the appendix to evaluate benefits options and clarify what you want to accomplish at the bargaining table.

FROM THE EMPLOYER'S SIDE OF THE TABLE

Benefits are a big factor in getting and keeping good workers. The objectives of providing benefits to employees include projecting a positive public image and convincing recruits to join the organization; increasing worker loyalty, morale, and motivation; and reducing unplanned turnover. Employees today have concerns about benefits portability, and before- and after-tax costs and advantages. Utilizing before-tax benefits makes employees' benefits dollars go further. A perquisite appeals only to those employees who are interested in that specific benefit; therefore, cafeteria plans are often seen as desirable by workers who are educated consumers. Companies must ensure that benefits are relevant and cost-effective for employees through ongoing program evaluation and fine-tuning.

Benefits are costly and represent a substantial employer investment on behalf of the workforce. Many benefits are regulated at the federal and/or state level; in some parts of the country, state requirements are more rigorous than federal regulations. Well-designed plans allow employers to leverage benefits allocations to provide for greater employee security and well-being, and workers can almost always obtain better coverage at lower cost through employer plans than privately. In many cases today, worker benefits increase the total payroll expense by an estimated 35 to 40 percent. Plan eligibility, coverage, contributions, and cost sharing requirements must be balanced with worker morale and welfare. Companies don't always do a good job of communicating the value of benefits plans; even today, otherwise savvy workers often take benefits for granted.

POINTS TO REMEMBER

+ Benefits programs are becoming more flexible in response to worker diversity.

+ Company-offered benefits most often include health-care plans, income protection insurance, death benefits, and retirement and termination payments.

+ It's important to understand benefits plans and the types and levels of coverage that are offered.

+ You must consider both your short-term and long-term needs and goals when evaluating and selecting benefits options.

+ Employees often take benefits programs for granted; however, they can add an estimated 35 to 40 percent to a company's payroll expense.

HEALTH-CARE INSURANCE

Medical benefits are a highly desirable—and therefore highly visible—benefit. It is customary for employers to offer a fixed choice of plans and levels of coverage; negotiation opportunity is usually greatest for programs that address wellness and returning to work after an illness. An influential national and state health-care regulatory climate will likely continue impacting and reshaping existing practices and plan designs.

Buying into health insurance and wellness is a responsibility shared by the employer and the employee. Health costs have escalated, due in part to past inflation, the aging of the population, increased utilization, greater use of "defensive medicine" in response to litigation, and the costs involved with caring for the uninsured.

In recent years, the trend has moved toward further cost shifting (passing a portion of expenses along) from employer to employee—higher employee contributions and lower benefits coverage. This trend is somewhat offset by increased flex dollars, the amount credited to employees to assist in purchasing protection or to compensate for opting out of coverage. In addition to premium payments, worker cost sharing is largely accomplished through deductibles, coinsurance, and out-of-pocket assessment amounts. A deductible is the amount an insured person is required to spend before the plan begins to pay benefits. Coinsurance is a percentage of the total expense as apportioned between the insured and the plan; for example, the plan pays 80 percent and the plan participant is responsible for the remaining 20 percent of the bill. "Out-of-pocket" prescribes the costs that the insured individual will incur for covered services within a plan year; usually this amount is some combination of the deductible, coinsurance, and/or copay. (Copay is a small payment made by the insured for a service received; for example, an office visit.) Deductibles and copays, out-of-pocket payments, and major medical triggers and maximums are significant considerations in evaluating medical insurance protection.

WHAT IS HEALTH-CARE INSURANCE ALL ABOUT?

Medical insurance generally involves an alphabet soup of plan types, coverages, and costs:

Types of Plans

When you have a choice, the plan type you select depends on your preference for freedom of choice or cost minimization. In general, less expensive options give you less control over your care. Plan types range from the traditional indemnity and comprehensive plans (fee-for-service plans, i.e., with payment for services occurring as expenses are incurred), to a variety of network plans that prepay for identified services at a specified amount.

Basic health insurance plans with supplemental coverage such as major medical generally have no deductible for hospital and surgery up to a certain amount. Once that amount is reached, major medical is invoked, with an accompanying deductible and coinsurance assessment, up to a predetermined 100 percent coverage floor. Major medical is often offered in tandem with basic medical, protecting the insured person from catastrophic medical expenses.

Comprehensive plans cover a wide range of provider services within one package. In contrast to basic plans, up-front deductible and coinsurance obligations generally kick in immediately upon initial expensing, prior to or in conjunction with the benefit being applied. Health maintenance organizations (HMOs) encourage preventive care. They are both providers and insurers of medical care and coverage. HMOs may be either group practice associations (GPAs), where physicians share common facilities, or individual practice associations (IPAs), which are composed of independent physicians who work from their own offices and are allied via service contracts.

A variety of managed-care vehicles have evolved, combining health-care cost financing and care delivery. The dual focus in managed care is on cost containment through utilization review and preventive care. Utilization review encompasses ongoing assessment of proposed treatments and charges for appropriateness and cost acceptability. Members in some plans can seek services in or out of their plan's network of doctors and hospitals, usually with the guidance of a gatekeeper, or primary care physician (PCP).

Out-of-network care will almost always cost the patient more than in-network care.

Plan types have matured or been modified to create additional options, such as point-of-service (POS) plans and preferred provider organization (PPO) networks of health-care providers. A POS plan is a network plan affording participants a somewhat limited amount of in-network choice, although the patient may obtain service outside the network at a reduced rate of coverage. A PPO is essentially an entity that represents its member providers, voluntarily offering competitive discounts to groups. Broadly speaking, the essential difference between a typical POS plan and a PPO is that the POS plan mandates participant affiliation with a primary care physician or gatekeeper, whereas the PPO generally does not.

Provider-sponsored organization (PSO) plans are formed by affiliations of independent hospitals and physicians.

Fee Structure

Non-HMOs are plans in which you pay (or the plan pays) for medical services *after* you receive them. Traditional fee-for-service plans allow the greatest freedom of provider selection and may be commercially insured, nonprofit (Blue Cross/Blue Shield) insured, or self-insured. Commercially insured programs are those that use a traditional insurance carrier. In a self-insured scenario, an employer elects to absorb a certain amount of the cost of employee health care, possibly through the creation of a voluntary employees' beneficiary association (VEBA) trust for payment of medical and other benefits. Self-insured structures usually carry a stop-loss provision, which limits employer-absorbed loss to a certain amount, with an insurance company writing responsibility for anything over that amount. While the employer assumes primary risk, insurance is carried for protection against large losses—individual claims or aggregates.

PPOs provide greater reimbursement for services performed within their provider community, with reduced reimbursement available for out-of-network services. HMOs charge a flat, prepaid "capitation" (per-person) fee for a specific group of services. Some HMOs allow for open-ended provider selection, where members can seek treatment outside of the HMO's provider network, but at increased cost.

Coverage

Generally, plans cover some portion of physician fees and hospital room and board, including "miscellaneous charges" such as nursing care and supplies, and surgical, X-ray and radiology, and laboratory charges. Plans will generally identify expenses that are excluded or for which coverage is limited. Some plans are now broadening their medical protection to include full or partial expense coverage for

* Routine physical examinations

* Substance abuse and mental and behavioral health

* Separate dental and orthodontic insurance and choice of plan/provider

* Vision/optical care, eye examinations, lenses, and frames

* Hearing/auditory care and hearing devices

* Alternative care, such as birthing centers, skilled nursing care facilities, home health care, and hospices

* Alternative medicine, such as acupuncture, chiropractic, massage therapy, and nutritionist regimens

* Prescription drugs

Many plans offer prescription drug cards, which provide a lower or flat out-of-pocket rate, usually for generic drugs, at selected pharmacies and mail-order distributors. Maintenance prescription drug programs often incorporate electronic claims processing and utilization review.

Employee Costs and Contributions

Most employees today pay for part of their medical benefits, often with pretax dollars. With each plan choice, the employee cost components— including copays, deductibles, coinsurance, out-of-pocket/inside plan expenses, dollar limits, and disaster protection—differ.

Spending Accounts

One of the more advantageous tax law provisions enables you to set aside pretax dollars for reimbursement of uninsured medical expenses in the form of a health care spending account. Currently, these accounts expire annually; at the end of the year you lose any money you haven't used for qualified medical purposes.

A recent innovation is the medical savings account (MSA). Also known as a premium conversion plan, MSAs supplement high-deductible medical plans by enabling you to set aside savings in a tax-exempt account to pay routine out-of-pocket medical expenses. Still experimental, MSAs are generally linked to a catastrophe plan to protect against major medical expenses. You can roll over your MSA savings, use the account to buy insurance independently, or use it to pay directly for care. Penalties are invoked for nonmedical spending.

Wellness and Fitness

Wellness programs bolster individual responsibility for health by emphasizing education, a healthy lifestyle, preventive care, risk assessments and screenings, and a variety of activities and incentive/disincentive programs to encourage sensible health practices. Approaches include annual physicals, health club membership fee reimbursement or payroll deduction convenience, and programs that provide information to heighten health awareness and advocate stress management and self-care.

Some companies extend health-care benefits to encompass return-to-work support following illness or extended leaves, ergonomic reviews to ensure that work areas and equipment setups are "user-friendly," and an on- or off-site clinic or clinic staffing.

HOW DOES HEALTH CARE INSURANCE AFFECT YOU?

With health-care costs continuing to capture national attention, the expense and adequacy of medical benefits are of critical interest to everyone these days. For those who have special needs themselves or family members with specific medical conditions, information about eligibility and qualifying events, coverage, and frequency of opportunity to change enrollment options is especially important.

Key legislative directives on behalf of workers who are experiencing changes in work or life status facilitate continuation of health insurance and alleviate the effects of losing a source of group health coverage. The Consolidated

Omnibus Budget Reconciliation Act of 1985 (COBRA) allows for the temporary extension of group health coverage that would otherwise be canceled following a qualifying event, such as termination of employment or divorce, for a specific period of time. The cost of COBRA coverage to the insured is almost always higher than when he or she was employed; typically, a COBRA participant does not enjoy the benefit of employer premium contributions but rather pays the full cost of group coverage plus a small administrative charge. But this may still be more affordable than individual coverage.

The Health Insurance Portability and Accountability Act of 1996 (HIPAA) eliminates a period of pending coverage for the recently hired, formerly insured individual in most—*but not all*—cases. It prohibits insurers and employers from imposing most waiting periods for coverage (or no more than 12 months' hiatus, if previously uninsured), denials of coverage for preexisting medical conditions, and arbitrary policy cancellations. HIPAA requires past employers to provide certification of previous health coverage and makes worker "job lock" (the inability to change jobs for fear of losing medical coverage) because of preexisting medical problems an almost obsolete notion. Some individuals have the opportunity to be insured under two programs: their employer's plan and, for example, a spouse's plan as well. Considering premium expenses, such a dual course of coverage is not always financially wise. Frequently, a coordination of benefits clause governs the order of coverage under two insurance plans. With standard coordination of benefits, the total allowable expense is equal to a maximum combined coverage from both plans, not to exceed 100 percent of covered charges. A nonduplication approach is similar to coordination of benefits, but it does not allow for higher benefits between plans.

Considerations in evaluating a medical plan may extend to the availability of insurance for children, stepchildren, grandchildren, live-in unmarried domestic partners, or dependent parents. Are there stay-duration limits in alternative-care facilities? What cost-containment provisions—such as hospital preadmission certification or testing, care monitoring and discharge and post-discharge planning, and insurance limitations—are in place? Is hospice care covered? Is there a lifetime benefit maximum?

You should also view medical plan protection in conjunction with a company's sick leave and disability plans—eligibility, waiting period requirements, pay amount and duration, and accumulation rules. Other questions to ask include whether medical plan conversion privileges are offered and under what conditions. Conversion is the right to purchase a private insurance policy without medical screening, within a certain time period following cancellation of group coverage.

FROM THE EMPLOYER'S SIDE OF THE TABLE

Selecting and managing employer-provided (employer-financed, at least in part) health insurance benefits is a continuing challenge. In addition to providing responsive coverage while managing costs, organizations must be vigilant and ensure adherence to compliance requirements.

Plans may be described as fully insured via a group contract placed with an insurance carrier, a network, or a nonprofit association; or self-insured, where the company assumes risk, usually to a certain limit, with risk above that ceiling insured by outside sources. Outsourcing plan administration to experienced third-party administrators (TPAs) with their resident technical expertise is one way for companies to handle plan management. An administrative services only (ASO) vendor arrangement is one in which claims processing is contracted out.

Cost-containment programs can introduce practices such as utilization review—an ongoing evaluation of plan coverage relative to services obtained—care charges, treatment practices, monitoring of services and care through individual case management, and restriction of patient access to care providers through plan design.

Employees too are conscious of the cost of health care today. Along with carefully packaged insurance benefits, medical spending accounts help employees manage their health insurance dollars more effectively, as do medical savings accounts (MSAs). The jury is still out on MSAs, however; the accounts may produce adverse selection, where participation in the accompanying high-deductible health insurance is not representative of the employee population as a whole. For example, those in poor health, with a higher likelihood of health-related claims, may more frequently select the broadest available amount of insurance protection, while people in good health, often the younger segment of the work population, elect lower levels of coverage or none at all.

Adequate health care is one of the major concerns of workers. As such, a thoughtfully crafted, professionally administered, well communicated health insurance plan is a banner recruiting tool. There are also any number of "nice-to-haves" that enhance basic or core medical coverage, some of which are relatively inexpensive to provide in a group context. The company's plan administrator will be able to define the leeway you may have, if any, to tailor health insurance coverage and wellness programs to an individual recruit's unique needs.

POINTS TO REMEMBER

- Health-care regulations and regulatory initiatives will continue to impact benefits.

- Health-care costs are escalating, and employees are bearing a higher percentage of these costs than they did in the past.

- Traditional health-care plans offer more flexibility in choosing care providers, but managed-care plans are almost always more affordable.

- Flexible spending accounts and medical savings accounts enable you to set aside money for medical costs while enjoying tax advantages.

- Employers are increasingly offering wellness programs, which promote individual responsibility for health.

- Choosing among medical and wellness benefits requires you to be an *informed* consumer and to consider many factors.

MEDICAL PLAN ANALYSIS

Use the following worksheet to evaluate the medical plan(s) offered by the employer at the time of the negotiation. You can use it again after you're hired to chart in detail the types and levels of coverage you need.

PLAN	PREMIUM	MEMBERSHIP	COSTS	COVERAGE	EXCLUSIONS
Provider and plan type/ coverage level	Monthly cost to employee after flex credit	Eligibility guide-lines/qualifying events	Noncovered costs/ copay/deductible/ coinsurance: Individual/ dependents Maximum out-of-pocket/ major medical trigger/plan maximum	Type and percent of expenses covered: Physician Hospital Mental health Dental Vision Hearing Alternative care Alternative medicine Prescription drugs Wellness Other	Coverage limits and exclusions
Plan A					

continues

continued

PLAN	PREMIUM	MEMBERSHIP	COSTS	COVERAGE	EXCLUSIONS
Plan A, continued					

PLAN	PREMIUM	MEMBERSHIP	COSTS	COVERAGE	EXCLUSIONS
Plan B					

continues

continued

PLAN	PREMIUM	MEMBERSHIP	COSTS	COVERAGE	EXCLUSIONS
Plan C					

INCOME PROTECTION AND REPLACEMENT

Income protection and replacement programs offer workers a measure of financial peace of mind. Knowing what coverage is available and choosing the right level of protection engenders a sense of security that contributes positively to morale. With this in mind, a candidate can point out reasonable need and mutual gain when negotiating for income protection.

Income protection and income replacement plans are forms of insurance and savings that allow workers to anticipate and proactively arrange for potentially large out-of-pocket expenditures and the continuation of living expenses under adverse conditions. These benefits assist employees in planning for standard-of-living maintenance and providing for large and/ or final expenses.

WHAT IS INCOME PROTECTION AND REPLACEMENT ALL ABOUT?

Income protection encompasses a number of options to ensure income continuation or replacement should a triggering event occur. Such events are usually health- or life-related. Sick pay is a benefit related to salary or hourly wage continuation. Employer policies vary regarding sick leave accrual and accumulation and rules regarding forfeiture, carryover, or sale of unused sick days. In addition to Social Security, unemployment insurance, and workers' compensation, income protection also includes short-term disability (STD), long-term disability (LTD), long-term health care, life insurance, liability, and miscellaneous other coverages.

Disability Benefits

Both short-term and long-term disability benefits are usually administered by a formula based on a percent of salary replacement. The plan will define eligibility, waiting period (if any), number of days earned or granted per specified period, term duration at 100 percent salary replacement and/or at reduced benefits, and coordination with sick days, workers' compensation, and Social Security benefits. Plan provisions may include continuation of service credit, savings/profit sharing credit accrual, and maintenance of health coverage during the period that the covered individual is receiving disability benefits.

Long-Term Care Insurance

People are living longer today and families are often less able to care for relatives who need assistance with the functions of daily living than was possible, even customary, in the past. Meeting the need for custodial care, long-term health care is a relatively new kid on the block. Long-term care insurance covers very specific maintenance care, at home or in a nursing or day-care facility, in the event of an incapacitating illness. Coverage for a spouse and even for parents may also be offered, sometimes independently of employee enrollment. This insurance typically offers financial assistance through periodic payment of a flat dollar amount for certain types of care required by people with chronic or longer-duration health problems under specific conditions. When the policy benefit is claimed by the insured, plan contribution or premium waiver provisions may be engaged. Other avenues of relief for families of those needing long-term care include care subsidies, spending accounts, referral programs, support groups, and community-participation opportunities.

Life Insurance

Life insurance is a frequently offered employment benefit, usually in the form of basic term life. There may or may not be a cost to the worker and the possibility of a conversion option in the case of termination of employment. Additional life insurance may also be offered, where the employee bears the entire cost of the expanded coverage on a voluntary basis.

Among the many forms of life insurance found in the workplace are universal life, group universal life, and split-dollar life insurance. Universal life contains an investment element through which a portioned cash value is accumulated; the employee generally pays the premiums. Split-dollar life is an arrangement in which the employer and employee share the expenses of the insurance and may also share in the equity and death benefits of the coverage. Policies covering accidental death and dismemberment, as well as business travel and 24-hour travel and accident policies, are also frequently available. Dependent life insurance and survivor income benefit insurance (SIBI), arranged as either a lump sum or periodic payments to the beneficiary, may be obtainable as well.

Other Income-Protection Plans

Companies in volatile industries sometimes extend supplemental unemployment benefits (SUBs) to their workers. Often as part of a union contract an employer will provide a benefit supplementing state-administered unemployment compensation to workers on temporary layoff.

Lastly, the nature of some jobs gives rise to inquiries regarding insurance against financial liability resulting from the execution of job duties. Some employers will offer director and officer insurance to protect against the risk of negative events, such as mismanagement or malpractice.

HOW DOES INCOME PROTECTION AND REPLACEMENT AFFECT YOU?

Loss of income can create a dramatic change in your security and standard of living. Having the opportunity to participate in income-protection programs can increase your peace of mind and contribute to your satisfaction with your new job.

You probably won't have much flexibility to negotiate income protection benefits. Generally, the plans and plan features offered by an employer are controlled and you need only choose whether to participate and at what level. But you should always ask questions! What are the restrictions in the accidental death and dismemberment plan? Can you purchase in-effect, split-dollar life insurance if you leave the employing company? Are there age-related coverage reductions to employer-sponsored life insurance upon retirement? Is the survivor income benefit structured as a tax-free death benefit?

In the final analysis, it is the responsibility of the employee to take care of his or her financial security. Have a good understanding of your benefits in the event of sickness and/or death. It is almost certain that you will experience some form of extended illness or disability during your career or lifetime. Income loss is a primary concern of most workers, and it's up to you to identify any gaps in your income protection. Many employers continue health and life insurance during periods of disability, but you will want to make sure you have the level of protection you need, based on your unique situation. In addition to mandated programs, cafeteria benefits plans and outside sources of coverage give workers a broader selection and more control over planning for income protection.

FROM THE EMPLOYER'S SIDE OF THE TABLE

Illness is a fact of life; consequently, most companies have a sick-pay policy to govern time off. Many plans allow employees to accrue sick days depending on length of service. Unfortunately, in some cases, employees view sick pay as an entitlement. Poorly designed plans may inadvertently create a reason for people to be out of work; for example, an uncapped accumulation of unused sick days, without exchange or forfeiture provisions, can promote misuse. To avert the potential for abuse, an organization with a relatively liberal sick-pay plan may require a doctor's note for an absence exceeding a certain consecutive number of days. Some employers even have spot awards or other recognition for attendance to discourage frivolous use of sick time. A new approach in the workplace is the "total time off" bank, combining sick days, vacation days, and holidays into a single block account for each employee, with rules that govern scheduling and use.

The short-term disability period is usually a span of five or six months; long-term disability benefits typically follow exhaustion of any short-term disability benefit. Long-term disability status screening occurs in two phases:

1. The affected worker can no longer perform his or her regular job; and

2. The worker can no longer perform any job.

The latter is intended to encourage rehabilitation.

Workers across major industry groups and occupations have access to a wide spectrum of levels and kinds of income coverage. Federally mandated programs—Social Security and unemployment compensation (delegated to and administered by the states)—and state-regulated workers' compensation form the income-protection base for most workers, around which employer-sponsored plans are wrapped. Mandatory programs represent a significant company expense; currently, organizations are required to pay all of the costs of unemployment and half of the Social Security assessment for their workers. Workers' compensation, administered at the state level, is also an employer-financed welfare benefit. In allocating benefit dollars, structuring a menu of choices that is sensitive to the needs of individual workers (such as employees who travel extensively for the organization or employees with family financial responsibilities) can be both cost-effective and program-enhancing.

POINTS TO REMEMBER

- ◆ Income-protection plans include sick leave, short-term disability, long-term disability, long-term health care, and life insurance.

- ◆ Short-term and long-term disability programs, which are usually based on a percentage of your base salary, are crucial to managing financial security.

- ◆ Many different forms of life insurance exist, not all of which are offered by every employer.

- ◆ Liability insurance is another form of income protection that employers may offer.

- ◆ Although you may not be able to negotiate too much in the way of income-replacement options, it is useful to understand them and ask questions.

- ◆ Responsibility for financial planning rests with the employee.

INCOME PROTECTION AND REPLACEMENT WORKSHEET

Use the following worksheet to review the income-protection and replacement plans offered by the company. Are benefits continued during a period of extended illness? What are the tax implications of the benefits offered? Consider whether it would be wise to look into obtaining or supplementing any of these coverages independently.

BENEFIT FEATURE	PRIORITY ITEM (✔)	RELATIVE POWER/ OPTIONS	EMPLOYER FLEXIBILITY	NOTES
Sick pay				
Short-term disability				
Long-term disability				
Long-term health care				

BENEFIT FEATURE	PRIORITY ITEM (✔)	RELATIVE POWER/ OPTIONS	EMPLOYER FLEXIBILITY	NOTES
Life insurance forms and coverages:				
Basic life				
Universal life				
Split-dollar				
Dependent life				
Other				
Supplemental and miscellaneous coverages:				
AD&D				
Business travel and 24-hour travel and accident				
Survivor income benefit				
SUBS				
Liability insurance				
Other				

continues

continued

BENEFIT FEATURE	PRIORITY ITEM (✔)	RELATIVE POWER/ OPTIONS	EMPLOYER FLEXIBILITY	NOTES
Outside sources of income protection and replacement				

RETIREMENT AND TERMINATION OF EMPLOYMENT

Most companies offer some sort of pension plan. You need to understand the many forms these plans can take before you enter negotiations, so that you can be sure you're making the right choices and providing adequately for your future.

Company pension payouts alone will not provide you with enough money to live comfortably in your retirement. Establishing the income sources for financial security in your retirement years is ultimately your responsibility.

Today's workers will have a number of jobs and perhaps several careers over their working lives. Many people are retiring early, only to begin new vocational pursuits. The era of lifetime employment with a single organization is over. Because of the current employment climate, separations and terminations are also an important point of discussion in job negotiations. You need to know what will happen to your retirement funds if you leave the company before you reach retirement age.

WHAT ARE RETIREMENT AND TERMINATION OF EMPLOYMENT ALL ABOUT?

Generally thought of as income deferred beyond the term of employment, retirement is funded through three main sources: Social Security, individual savings, and company pension plans. Employment-based pension retirement income, payment that begins at a minimum age after an individual leaves active service with a company, may take the form of a lump sum or an annuity and is usually reduced if payouts start before a certain age. Annuities are periodic payments made to a retiree over a fixed period of time.

Preretirement planning is of heightened importance today for all workers. Some companies offer assistance in preparing for retirement, either in–house or through an external vendor. Retirement-planning programs educate workers about retirement issues and increase preretirement employee morale. These programs help individuals examine their present lifestyle as well as their desired postretirement standard of living, and the tax and financial implications of decisions related to retirement.

Retirement Plans

Pension plans are carefully regulated by the government. The Employee Retirement Income Security Act of 1974 (ERISA) enacted radical legislation of pension plan coverage eligibility, vesting, funding, and plan-termination rules; and it established fiduciary standards for private pension plans. Following from ERISA, the Pension Benefit Guaranty Corporation (PBGC) provides pension-plan termination insurance. Federal legislation encourages benefit plan access for a diverse workforce base, rather than any one segment. Compliance with government requirements allows for favorable tax treatments; for example, pretax contributions for employees and timely tax deductions for employers. There are rules and restrictions regarding early distributions and withdrawals from retirement plan savings. Post-ERISA legislation, while not as sweeping, has continued to modify the regulatory environment for pension plans.

Pension plans are broadly categorized as either defined-benefit (in which you know up front how much the payout will be) or defined-contribution (in which the payout will vary).

The type of plan, the funding and formula, the amount of the company's contribution, and a schedule of employee vesting are key to determining the plan's vitality. Vesting, the right to retain that portion of the plan benefits accrued even if employment is terminated before retirement, may be immediate, may follow a waiting period, or may be phased in. The employee's contribution, if any, is always fully vested.

Still most common, a defined-benefit plan is one in which the benefit is known. Not an individual account, it is generally based on the accumulation of pension credits by means of a formula of a percentage of salary and years of service, and it pays out either a predetermined lump sum or a flat-dollar-amount annuity at retirement. Alternatively, some formulas pay a certain dollar amount per year of service, which may increase the likelihood of retirement at a relatively early age. Many defined-benefit plans contain a Social Security integration provision. Since Social Security replaces a larger portion of pay for lower-paid workers, companies make an effort to accommodate higher-paid employees through one of two methods. First, the company might offset some of the employer-paid portion of a worker's Social Security benefit through a pension reduction.

Second, the company could use a step rate to calculate pensions, where the percentage of salary being paid out increases incrementally.

With the high mobility of workers today, a cash-balance plan alternative has emerged. This is still a defined-benefit plan, but it appears to be a hybrid of the defined-contribution and defined-benefit models. Typically, it is an individual account within a plan, holding a percent of pay relative to years of service, earning compounded interest, and resulting in earlier significant benefit accrual, paid out as a lump sum.

Defined contribution individual account plans, often but not always designed to supplement defined-benefit plans, include savings or thrift with a company match; deferred profit sharing, with the employee being credited with an apportioned share; and money purchase plans, where participants garner annuities through predetermined formulary employer contributions to individual accounts.

Defined-contribution plans stipulate employer and/or employee contributions, but they do not guarantee a benefit amount. Where applicable, for example, in money purchase and 401(k) plans, and within company-established parameters, the worker may guide the investment of the defined-contribution funds.

Most 401(k) or incentive savings plans have eligibility requirements. Generally the employee must be with the company a certain length of time before he or she is permitted to participate in the plan. The employee's savings may be combined with a company contribution or "match" (which matches a percentage of the employee's contributions, up to a prescribed limit). Money in a 401(k) plan is generally portable—employee contributions and the "vested" part of the employer match aren't forfeited when the employee leaves the company.

Withdrawal of funds from a 401(k) is restricted and conditional. These plans allow the participant to defer taxes through shifting part of the before-tax salary into savings and investments. Plan features generally include investment options in a spectrum of individual stocks, bonds, and mutual funds; trade conventions; contribution ceilings; and loan guidelines.

Occasionally an employer may facilitate employee participation in a variable annuity, where the value accumulated and paid out is not fixed but varies, most often in accordance with the fortunes of the investment market. For employees working in the nonprofit sector, 403(b) tax-sheltered annuities (TSAs) enable the purchase of annuities on a pretax basis to supplement pension plans. Smaller employers may offer a simplified employer plan (SEP), where contributions may be made by the employer up to a federally regulated maximum. Individuals can also participate in individual retirement account (IRA) savings, using either pre- or post-tax dollars, depending on the individual situation.

Employee Share Ownership Plans (ESOPs) are also considered defined contribution plans. ESOPs and stock purchase plans, where employees buy shares of company stock often discounted to below market value, serve the dual purpose of encouraging employee ownership in the company and helping workers plan for retirement. Design and funding of ESOPs with company allocation of stock for employees vary. Such plans may, for example, be in the form of a trust or a portion of stock reserved for employees' retirement as a percent of payroll.

Mandatory retirement has been modified or abolished in most cases. On the other hand, early retirement may be a prerogative for some workers. The impact on benefits, continuation of insurance coverage, option of and formula for early retirement payment, and availability of a retention bonus plan need to be considered in today's environment of constant change and downsizing. Organizations are more frequently offering "stay" bonuses in the face of imminent downsizing, in order to hold on to the services of valued employees through a certain period that is critical to the continuation of business.

Health insurance coverage is an important consideration when planning for retirement. Most employer medical plans are designed to be integrated with and supplement Medicare when a worker is eligible for it. To manage cost, some companies are taking a defined approach or using an index to cap the subsidy for medical premiums for their retirees; others are increasing premiums for retired workers. Some employers extend continued access to employee assistance programs, fitness facilities, and other employee services after retirement.

In addition to normal and early retirement, special-opportunity programs— contained periods or windows offering enhanced early retirement or retirement incentives—may be made available to employees on occasion in response to business need.

Workers may be able to phase in retirement in some organizations, either by working a reduced schedule or by participating in a retiree job bank, where retirees are employed to fill temporary positions in the company. In these circumstances, benefits are usually continued, although pension payout may be placed on hold. Many retirees choose to remain active through postretirement consulting.

Involuntary Termination

In planning for involuntary termination, an understanding of employer definitions around job loss, such as termination for good reason, nonextension by the company, or without cause by the company is advisable. Review the company's salary-continuation and severance plan, if there is one, and determine the plan's rules. Clarify whether an employee who is involuntarily terminated and eligible for severance can elect to take severance payments in a lump sum. Keep in mind that under certain circumstances, an employee who is involuntarily separated may be able to obtain liquidating damages, such as accelerated vesting or cashout, payout gross-ups (where the employee's tax liability is added to the payout), and work-related relocation reimbursement.

Special arrangements may be made in case of termination due to a change in control of the company. "Golden parachute" financial support and benefits often protect senior executives; "tin parachutes" sometimes take care of all, or all salaried, employees in the event of a takeover, mitigating the effects of the ownership change.

Many employers underwrite outplacement assistance in the case of job loss, sometimes in combination with severance pay. Plans differ in their eligibility guidelines, the nature of termination to qualify for assistance, term, support components, inclusion of work preference testing and counseling, and whether facilitation is provided by an in-house or external vendor source. These programs offer advice regarding unemployment and guidance in seeking a new job. Their presence lessens to some extent the impact of termination, boosting the morale of both the separated and the retained population.

Some organizations have policies regarding unused vacation and sick time upon termination—you may or may not be paid for any remaining vacation or sick time when you leave.

Another issue related to termination is the company's rehire policy; for instance, are former employees, when rehired, granted credit for past service? Some employers have policies regarding leaves of absence and buy-backs as well.

"Portability" of Retirement Funds

Defined-benefit pension plans, where the employer promises the employee a certain formula-based annuity, may not be readily transferable. Pension portability is most often found in defined-contribution plans such as a 401(k). Generally, upon termination before normal retirement age, defined-contribution pension moneys are either rolled over or taken as a lump sum, which may lead to tax penalties if the employee does not reinvest the payout comparably within a specified period of time.

In response to increased worker mobility, there is a new concept surfacing that pension benefits "follow the person," that is, be ceded to the worker through present-value withdrawal and transfer and possibly through service credit reciprocity agreements between certain affiliated employers.

HOW DO RETIREMENT AND TERMINATION OF EMPLOYMENT AFFECT YOU?

Retirement used to be something companies designed on behalf of long-term employees. Today, retirement planning is the responsibility of the individual, working in partnership with the employer. Know the cash value of any present pension benefit in preparation for negotiations.

Find out the employing organization's pension plan type, formula, and the definition of covered pay. Clarifying questions to ask, depending on the nature of the plan, might include:

- Is the plan insured?
- What is the vesting convention?
- What is the normal retirement age?
- Are bonus awards included in pension payout calculations?

- Does the plan offer investment choices?

- What are the plan restrictions around investments?

- Is the 401(k) match determined by company performance? If so, how is performance measured?

- Is the savings plan account forfeited under any circumstances?

- What happens to benefits when an employee retires?

- Is there an early retirement subsidy?

- Is there a Social Security integration in the pension determination?

- Is there a cost-of-living adjustment built into the retirement plan?

Negotiate for immediate or accelerated vesting of pension rights. Older, experienced workers may also be able to negotiate for additional years of service and/or age for pension calculations. Sometimes, an annuity can make up the difference in the event of pension benefits lost when changing jobs.

In the case of involuntary termination, is there a severance program or a combination salary continuation or call-back period and severance plan? Other negotiables include additional weeks of severance pay and an extension of benefits coverage and payment periods. Is there a benefits buy-back option in the event of rehire?

In instances of both voluntary and involuntary termination, a clear understanding of applicable trade secrets agreements, confidentiality, and other restrictions is essential.

FROM THE EMPLOYER'S SIDE OF THE TABLE

The "three-legged stool" retirement model depicts three sources of income for retiring employees, pragmatically moving workers away from being overly dependent on Social Security to creating a more reasonable balance between Social Security, pension, and individual savings. The type of pension plan and retirement savings offered often reflects the philosophy of the employing organization. An established, more paternalistic company may prefer the security and predictability of a defined-benefit plan for its employees, where payout is not directly related to business or pension investment results. A participative management may select the partnership approach inherent in deferred profit-sharing plans. Savings and thrift plans rely on employee initiative and motivation. Supplemental plans improve retirement resources for employees, and along with retirement plans, they are an attractive benefit to most workers. Occasionally, administrative costs for managing employee 401(k) plans and similar investments are unusually high and may merit examination. Holding an early retirement provision is sometimes advantageous to the employer; managing turnover through attrition may be an acceptable alternative to layoffs.

In some instances, voluntary resignation—should a new employment relationship not work out as well as initially anticipated—may be planned for at the time of hire. Seasoned recruits may also inquire as to whether involuntary termination of employment can be addressed proactively, particularly in turnaround situations or in industries or professions with traditionally (supply- and demand-driven) high turnover.

POINTS TO REMEMBER

- Even though companies provide retirement funding programs, overall retirement planning is the responsibility of the individual.

- Company-sponsored retirement plans can be either defined-benefit (a set payout) or defined-contribution (a variable payout, as in a 401[k]) plans.

- With fewer people having lifetime jobs with a single employer, pension portability is extremely important.

- The voluntary and involuntary termination programs offered by some companies help support employees in transition.

SEPARATION BENEFITS WORKSHEETS

Use the following worksheets to assess what retirement security you will be able to build through the employer. Review the plans with special attention to eligibility, vesting, and formula provisions. Think through the tax implications of various alternatives.

Voluntary Separation and Retirement

BENEFIT FEATURE	PRIORITY ITEM (✔)	RELATIVE POWER/ OPTIONS	EMPLOYER FLEXIBILITY	NOTES
Defined-benefit plan				
Cash balance plan				
Defined-contribution individual account plan				
Stock/stock purchase				
Other supplemental plan				

continues

Voluntary Separation and Retirement, continued

BENEFIT FEATURE	PRIORITY ITEM (✓)	RELATIVE POWER/ OPTIONS	EMPLOYER FLEXIBILITY	NOTES
Savings and thrift				
Profit sharing				
Money purchase				
401(k)				

BENEFIT FEATURE	PRIORITY ITEM (✔)	RELATIVE POWER/ OPTIONS	EMPLOYER FLEXIBILITY	NOTES
403(b)				
Variable annuity				
Financial/retirement planning				
Reduced work schedule/ postretirement employment				

continues

Involuntary Separation and Termination

BENEFIT FEATURE	PRIORITY ITEM (✔)	RELATIVE POWER/ OPTIONS	EMPLOYER FLEXIBILITY	NOTES
Salary continuance/ severance pay plan				
Lump-sum severance				
Golden/tin parachute triggers				
Benefits conversion				

Voluntary and Involuntary Separations

BENEFIT FEATURE	PRIORITY ITEM (✔)	RELATIVE POWER/ OPTIONS	EMPLOYER FLEXIBILITY	NOTES
Retention bonus				
Outplacement services				
Medical coverage/ benefits continuation				
Life insurance				
Pension portability				
Benefits payouts				

continues

Voluntary and Involuntary Separations, continued

BENEFIT FEATURE	PRIORITY ITEM (✔)	RELATIVE POWER/ OPTIONS	EMPLOYER FLEXIBILITY	NOTES
Confidentiality agreement				
Proprietary rights				
Other restrictions				
Rehire policy				

CHAPTER 12

Additional Employee Benefits

NEGOTIATION VIEWPOINT

Already representing a considerable portion of the total compensation package, benefits are increasingly a factor in the current employment environment. Changing workforce values are reflected in the complexity of the overlap between work and personal life today. The employee benefits your company offers can make a big difference in your life at work and outside of work. During negotiations, you can, to some extent, determine the benefits you will obtain.

WHAT ARE ADDITIONAL EMPLOYEE BENEFITS ALL ABOUT?

In addition to financial compensation, health and income insurance and protection, and retirement, many employers have put adjunct benefits in place to further provide for the well-being of their workforce. Additional employee benefits include relocation programs, work and family programs, and executive and supplemental benefits. While not technically in the benefits family, travel and business expense policies are close cousins of benefits in that they are part of the company work environment standard.

HOW DO ADDITIONAL EMPLOYEE BENEFITS AFFECT YOU?

It may be possible to negotiate job-related relocation assistance, work environment flexibility, financial assistance for professional development, and supportive arrangements for meeting personal responsibilities. In companies where entertainment and travel are part of the work protocol, standards and reimbursement programs that help employees cope with these aspects of doing business are worth discussing. Executive and supplemental benefits are often made available for senior staff, and some of these may serve as models for similar benefits being more inclusively extended within some organizations.

There is a new team environment in the workplace—a shift from paternalism to partnership, toward more humanistic and holistic work policies and a renewed emphasis on career development. Many programs are mutually beneficial; for example, employers often sponsor or underwrite job-related training and education. Such development helps employees prepare for new jobs, and also leads to increased contribution and job satisfaction. Socially desirable and business-smart, employee benefits positively affect morale and worker commitment.

FROM THE EMPLOYER'S SIDE OF THE TABLE

Benefits are no longer fixed, or confined to "the basics" an employer is required to provide. More often today, companies are responding to workforce requisites with additional benefits that can be modified to fit various circumstances. Employees need to be where the business needs them to be; relocation and business entertainment and travel are a fundamental part of the way some companies do business. At the same time, employees must juggle the demands and conditions of work, keep an eye on their professional development, and adhere to their personal life values. It often makes good business sense for the company to provide support in many or all of these areas. A final note: The need for competitive executive compensation and adaptive supplemental benefits has not diminished in today's scramble for the leadership edge and expertise necessary to capture and maintain market share.

POINTS TO REMEMBER

- ◆ Additional company-offered benefits may include relocation assistance, work and family programs, business travel and entertainment reimbursement, and executive benefits.

- ◆ Worker benefit plans can give you the opportunity to structure the climate and conditions within which work is undertaken and performed.

- ◆ The right benefits programs improve employee morale and productivity and encourage desired worker loyalty and commitment.

RELOCATION ASSISTANCE

The purpose of relocation programs is to cover major work-related moving expenses and thus ease employee transition costs and concerns. Relocation assistance for newly hired individuals and those already employed encourages the employee population to be more open to mobility and allows the employer to maintain greater hiring and organizational flexibility.

Relocation packages are generally standardized at large companies, but there is still room for negotiation in some cases. Smaller and midsize organizations are less likely to offer substantial relocation assistance than larger companies are. However, relocation is costly, and you can often negotiate some reimbursement.

Many companies have work sites in multiple locations within state lines, across the country, and even international settings. If an employer provides relocation cost differentials for major metropolitan areas, these generally apply to both home-purchase and leasing transactions.

WHAT IS RELOCATION ASSISTANCE ALL ABOUT?

Relocation packages are designed with the intention of keeping employees "whole" and encouraging a willingness to move on behalf of the employer. Relocation programs also aid in employee retention and therefore reduce hiring and training expenses.

Policies for newly hired and transferred employees may differ. A new employee relocating at the time of hire is usually offered a less "rich" package; approximately one month's salary is sometimes a rule of thumb for total new-hire moving expenses. Most often, travel and the cost of moving furnishings, and possibly temporary housing and furniture storage, is considered appropriate for new-hire relocation reimbursement. Seasoned professionals may be given greater move support than a recent graduate; an individual filling a senior management position can expect to enjoy substantial relocation assistance.

Relocation packages typically include some or all of the following elements:

Lump-Sum Reimbursement

More and more these days, relocation assistance comes in the form of a lump-sum. Lump-sum reimbursement offers you the most latitude and choice in handling the move. The lump sum may be negotiated to incorporate a tax allowance to offset any tax impact to you. From the employer's viewpoint, lump sums lessen administration and associated costs.

Sometimes a small additional "miscellaneous" or discretionary payment is also provided to cover one-time incidental move-related expenses.

Existing Home Sale

The employing organization may assist with the cost of selling existing property through equity and bridge loans, and by helping with loan interest and mortgage fees. The company may also reimburse you for such selling costs as appraisal, advertising, inspections, broker and attorney fees, transaction fees, taxes, and losses of principal upon disposal of property in depressed housing markets. The company may contract with a real estate firm to provide you with home sale and disposition assistance, such as third-party home purchase plans, and/or premarketing advice, loss on sale evaluations, and sale administration. A self-marketing bonus incentive, often a small percentage of the sale price, may be offered to encourage homeowners to actively participate in selling the home. In the case of rental, the company may pay the charges for breaking a lease.

House Hunting

Relocation expenses may also include airfare and car rental for house-hunting trips for the employee and spouse, home-finding counseling and assistance, a lodging and meals allowance, child care, and temporary living expenses for a period of time. If the employee moves ahead of the family, the company may arrange for periodic trips home in the interim before the move is accomplished.

Moving

Reimbursable moving expenses may include costs for household goods, automobiles, specialty goods such as antiques and other valuables, move insurance, a trip home to supervise the move, family travel, packing and unpacking, temporary housing, furniture rental, and goods storage costs. The company may also provide move-coordination resources.

New Home

The company may consider reimbursing you for the cost of renting/leasing or purchasing a home. It may provide allowances to subsidize a portion of rent or to be applied to home-purchase costs such as mortgage discount fees, title search and insurance, taxes, attorney fees and legal costs, settlement fees, home inspection and warranty, and environmental surveys and tests.

Other special programs some companies provide include mortgage loan consulting, mortgage interest variance or differential programs, down payment assistance or guarantees, and reimbursement of the temporary cost of carrying two homes—utilities, maintenance, taxes and insurance, and interest payments. Some companies assist their workers with mortgage loans, either directly or through credit unions or other institutions.

International Relocation

International relocation is highly specialized and ideally includes cross-cultural training and resources to familiarize employees and their families with the new area's cultural and business norms. Destination services may provide help with paperwork, licenses, legalities and work authorizations, language training, education, and medical resources.

HOW DOES RELOCATION ASSISTANCE AFFECT YOU?

The availability of relocation assistance enables you to expand your job search geographically by making the transition to a new city easier. Often your first concern is moving and finding and setting up a new household; this is a sizeable up-front expense, as well as a major investment of time. Good relocation programs alleviate much of the worry and burden of moving, freeing you to concentrate on your new job functions with minimal disruption. Relocation support also goes a long way in easing the emotional stress of family members who must deal with new schools, new friends, and a new community. A spouse may benefit correspondingly from job-search assistance in the new location in order to make your whole family comfortable with the move decision.

Research the current home sales market and the cost of living in the new location before negotiations take place. A real estate agent who specializes in relocation can help you gather this information. A higher cost of living in the new location may affect your standard of living and home-buying power considerably.

During negotiations, ask the employer for a written summary of what moving expenses will be covered. Also ask about reimbursement limits. If the company uses a generic or standard statement of policy for relocation, be sure to expand on it to cover any additional support that you have negotiated.

During the move, you must keep careful records of your expenses so that you can be fairly reimbursed. You need to keep track of your expenditures and reimbursements for tax purposes as well. Most organizations have an accounting system and forms to assist with this task.

FROM THE EMPLOYER'S SIDE OF THE TABLE

Even though some employers are cutting back or eliminating expansive relocation packages, the overriding business priority is still to have the right people in the right place at the right time to do business. Targeted relocation assistance goes a long way toward making this possible. Moving is not only expensive, it is stressful to workers and their families. With today's dual-career families, the "trailing spouse" issue may give a highly qualified candidate pause in considering a job-related move. A recruiting advantage, relocation support can help a company attract workers with the valuable skills it needs and locate them where they can best contribute to the success of the business.

Evaluate the business need to relocate a recruit or transfer an individual shortly after hire. In general, any or all costs associated with moving may be covered at the employer's discretion. When a company has occasion to move its people frequently, it sometimes pays to have well-planned company-owned or leased temporary housing in place to facilitate relocation. Get good tax advice when structuring a relocation offer to maximize the advantages of this benefit for both the company and the new hire. Relocation reimbursement is generally considered taxable income to the recipient. In turn, certain moving costs may be deductible.

POINTS TO REMEMBER

- Be prepared for moving expense negotiations by researching the home sales market and cost of living in the new location.

- Lump-sum expense offset, as opposed to itemized expenses, is a growing trend in relocation.

- Relocation packages offered to new hires usually aren't as generous as the ones offered to transferred employees.

- Expenses that may be eligible for reimbursement include house-hunting costs, moving expenses, and the costs of selling and renting/buying a home.

- Careful records of all move-related expenses should be kept, both for reimbursement and for tax purposes.

- Consider and plan for the significant impact of relocation on family members and extended family.

RELOCATION ASSISTANCE WORKSHEET

Use this worksheet to analyze moving expenses and the employing company's move support and determine whether moving makes sense in your situation. Be sure you understand any tax consequences of the relocation benefit.

BENEFIT FEATURE	PRIORITY ITEM (✔)	RELATIVE POWER/ OPTIONS	EMPLOYER FLEXIBILITY	NOTES
Lump-sum allowance/ expense offset				
Current location, real estate market				
Existing home sale expenses				
Temporary housing				
House-hunting expenses				
Moving expenses				

continues

continued

BENEFIT FEATURE	PRIORITY ITEM (✔)	RELATIVE POWER/ OPTIONS	EMPLOYER FLEXIBILITY	NOTES
New location, real estate market, and cost of living				
New home expenses				
Other costs				
Family members' concerns				
Record-keeping and reimbursement protocol				

BALANCING WORK AND PERSONAL LIFE

Employees are beginning to assess their lifestyle needs, restructure their office hours, and enjoy the freedom to rearrange their schedules in response to individual and family priorities. Work arrangements, education, and personal/family life management are often areas where employers are most receptive to negotiation in order to attract and retain good workers and maintain a high level of employee commitment and morale.

The diversity of the workforce requires employer flexibility, an understanding of the differences in people, and awareness of the individuality of employee lifestyles and concerns. The ensuing good public and employee relations aids in worker motivation and increases productivity through reduced absenteeism and greater focus on the job. Diversity in all its expressions is good business.

WHAT IS BALANCING WORK AND PERSONAL LIFE ALL ABOUT?

Balance is about a company's recognition of and accommodation of its employees' personal life goals, needs, and wants. It's also about company programs and policies, particularly with regard to working arrangements, pay for time not worked, and time off without pay. The venues and variables are many.

The Work Environment and Working Conditions

When, where, and how people perform their work can have a significant impact on their productivity. Issues such as flexible scheduling, time-off policies, and a pleasant and convenient work atmosphere are continually of interest to employees.

Alternative Scheduling and Working Arrangements

Hours at work do not necessarily equal commitment. In fact, rigid rules and regulations regarding the hours and conditions of work can be counterproductive. Employees have a right to expect to be treated as adults who take ownership of their career and their work duties and who have legitimate responsibilities outside of work that do not negate, and are not inconsistent with, serious job and career orientation.

Days and hours of work are no longer the traditional eight-hours-a-day, five-days-a-week structure. Flexible time programs, such as compressed work weeks, alternative work schedules—to adjust for school hours and job sharing, for example—are now common practice and among the most popular benefits on employees' radar screens these days.

Flexible schedules meet the needs of workers with family obligations, students, retirees, and others. Morale and worker engagement seem to be high where alternate staffing arrangements are available. Flextime has been characterized as contributing to increased productivity and customer satisfaction. In contemplating an adapted schedule, keep in mind that the ability to be self-directed and the discipline to work independently are the hallmarks of a successful flextime worker.

When employees are working flexible hours, communication is of heightened importance. Information must be disseminated and meetings and training planned with these schedules in mind. Sometimes there is an impact on vacations and holidays. Benefits may be prorated when the time worked is less than full time. Record-keeping may be somewhat more cumbersome for the company. Parties should thoroughly document flexible work agreements, particularly those that are unique, in writing and invoke a trial period to evaluate the arrangement.

Flextime technically indicates a full-time position in which the hours worked are either staggered around a core time period or fully nonstandard. A compressed work week is full time but fewer than five days per week; for example, four 10-hour days or three 12-hour days.

Examples of variable work weeks include summer hours (where, for instance, employees might have Friday afternoons off in exchange for working those hours elsewhere in the week) and an alternating biweekly schedule of five days per week and four days per week, so that every other weekend is a three-day weekend.

Part-time regular work is generally a schedule of fewer than 35 to 40 hours per week and implies a proportionately reduced workload. Job sharing describes two or more individuals sharing one (usually full-time) position. Management must develop clarity around job responsibilities and administer pay comparably for comparable work in job shares.

Communication, work coordination, and teamwork are especially critical in a job-share agreement. The overlap often yields better coverage overall than a single worker can provide, and complimentary skill sets can prove advantageous to all parties.

Telecommuting and working at home, whether full-time, part-time, or occasional, is becoming widely accepted. Many nondesk jobs require that some paperwork be processed; the ability to do this in the field, usually by means of a laptop computer, is quite common today. In addition, the advent of the computer age is making it possible for "cottage industry" work to stage a comeback. Work at home can facilitate productivity gains through the obvious efficiencies around commuting and convenience and the ability to better meet personal life obligations, and also through firm worker commitment to making the flexible arrangement work. With the right equipment, support, and good communication, working at home is making a significant contribution to the new wave of worker flexibility.

Telecommuting is not for everyone. Performing work at home requires that you be very disciplined and self-directed. In addition, you will be losing some of the interaction and socialization of work that many people enjoy. Often, a combination of working at home and in an office setting is most appealing.

Another less traditional work option is independent contracting. Independent contractors are self-employed consultants doing freelance work generally not performed by company employees, and they are hired for a specified period of time. They are external to the organization's workforce, engaged to accomplish a specific task or project. Independent contractor status is federally regulated. In most cases, freelancers will not receive company-paid or subsidized benefits from the contracting organization.

Time Off

Paid time off includes the vacation plan (with vacation days often increasing in number along with years of service), the number of paid holidays, and the mix of designated holidays and discretionary days and personal time. Pay for breaks and rest periods, wash and clean-up time, and scheduled shutdown periods are other instances of time off with pay.

Plans define accrual and how much, if any, earned vacation time can be carried over from one year to the next, as well as whether an employee is required to take time off in specific minimum or maximum increments. Plans also usually spell out the number of any days paid for family illness, bereavement, and military leave. Occasionally, there is an opportunity to negotiate or qualify for additional days off, up to a company-determined maximum.

There may be a practice regarding compensation for unused vacation time, such as vacation buying/selling, pay in lieu of vacation, or trade-offs for unused accumulated sick time. Some organizations create an all-purpose leave bank of paid time off, to be allocated at worker discretion, with employer consent; for example, the time can be divided between vacation, illness, and need to care for an ill child or parent. A very limited number of companies offer a plan where, after a certain number of years of service, a one-time additional period of paid time off is granted to allow employees to recharge; a few offer the opportunity for sabbaticals. Sabbaticals usually require a specific objective, for example, continuing education, social or volunteer projects, or professional renewal. In both of these instances, it is important to be clear about whether and what benefits will continue.

Unpaid leave, that is, time off without pay, is available under certain circumstances by law and may be further extended under company policy. In the instance of unpaid personal or family leave, certain health and benefits coverages generally are continued. With few exceptions, if you have worked for 12 months and at least 1250 hours in a company of 50 or more employees, the Family and Medical Leave Act (FMLA) legislates up to 12 weeks of unpaid leave per year. Employees may use this time for the medical emergencies or serious illness of a parent, spouse, child, or self, and for maternal/paternal birth leave, adoption, and foster child arrangements, with reinstatement—return to work to the same or equivalent job with the same pay and benefits. Generally, advance notification is required and companies have an authorization process to guide supervisors and employees in effecting a family leave arrangement.

Any extended time off work should trigger questions regarding benefits coverage and continuation. Organizational policies differ with regard to continuation of benefits while on leave. Health insurance generally is continued, but not all organizations maintain the same liberal array and level of benefits coverage for workers on leave. Some companies keep most benefits in place but do not grant service credit during the leave period; others continue selected plan components but put some components on hold; still others continue benefits but do not subsidize costs. Since benefits protection is such an important part of the employment relationship, any changes resulting from a period of time away from work must be clearly understood.

Work Atmosphere
Most of us work best in an environment that is safe, clean, orderly, and contains the furniture and equipment we need to do our job.

Perquisites broadly encompass the privileges (not all of which are always reserved for top management) of job title and accompanying executive status, office ambiance and style of furniture, preferred parking, upgraded personal computer and state-of-the-art technical equipment, and many other extras, as well as enhanced traditional benefits.

Other representative aspects of the work atmosphere are organized recreation programs, smoking policy, casual dress tolerance, and other such customs.

Acceptance of relaxed work attire, sometimes confined to "casual Fridays" or areas of a business where there is reduced public interaction, is a way in which companies are meeting worker desires for a less formal, more comfortable work atmosphere. Smoke-free workplaces are becoming the norm today, acknowledging not only the health implications of smoking but also the right of nonsmokers to enjoy good air quality in the workplace. Many companies, recognizing the need to maintain and bolster morale, encourage workers to socialize by underwriting employee club activities, subsidizing sports teams, and organizing social events such as company outings.

In every environment, workplace safety programs are important to both employers and the labor force. Employers may make provision for special or protective clothing to workers. The company often supplies or pays for required safety equipment, such as protective eyewear, clothing, or shoes. Occasionally, an employee may have a medical condition that justifies additional or tailored safeguards in the workplace.

The location of facilities and physical workspace and whether it is a remote workplace removed from the central building or the corporate headquarters are considerations. Practical concerns may include the adjacency of employee conveniences, such as an ATM, routine car care, dry cleaning, shoe repair, videos, groceries, drug store, and so forth. Some employers even offer employee access to concierge services for doing errands. Workers often also want to know whether and what recreational facilities are available on and off the premises.

With today's longer workdays, ways of dealing with meals come under new examination. Both time and cost are factors. It is not unusual for employees who are working under special circumstances, such as late hours or off location, to be furnished meals, both for efficiency and in acknowledgement of their service.

Are subsidized or courtesy meals, take-out, or microwave and refrigerator available to employees and under what circumstances? Has a dining room and/or cafeteria been established in the building or nearby? If there is a company cafeteria, is wellness taken into consideration and are healthy food alternatives part of the menu?

Parking and parking privileges are a frequent employee concern, especially in urban areas. Transportation and commuting issues include both time and convenience factors. Of interest are free or reduced parking rates, full or partial parking expense reimbursement, reserved spaces, indoor/outdoor vehicle housing (and information about any time or access restrictions), and employee and vehicle safety. Other considerations are the accessibility and suitability of van pools and whether discounted public transportation passes are available.

Lifelong Learning and Learning Organizations

The importance of continuing professional currency and growth cannot be overemphasized. Employer sensitivity to the need for ongoing management and employee development through in-house and vendor training programs and education assistance plans is key. Programs may encompass direct payment of tuition to an external teaching institution, reimbursement for approved coursework and textbook expenses, or reduced tuition agreements. Subsidies may cover required continuing-education units, technical certificates and licensing, and support of professional memberships and activities that lead to job skill enrichment. Some employers offer career counseling to their employees, helping them identify future work roles and plan development. Career development directly impacts an individual's opportunity for professional advancement, and future employability and value in the workplace.

Some companies have a philosophy of promotion from within the company. These organizations and others may develop employees through job rotations or community assignments, encouraging the broadening of knowledge and skills through new work experiences. Qualified workers whose skills are continually being developed or enhanced are more likely to make a commitment not only to themselves and their professional community, but also to their career within a particular industry and to the employer who encourages development. This commitment translates to higher morale, and thus higher productivity.

In addition to supporting lifelong learning for the employee, some organizations promote education for the employee's family. Certain employers, particularly teaching institutions, offer dependent scholarships and reimbursement for dependent tuition and textbooks. Some employers support development of technological literacy for the employee's entire family through a loan to buy a computer (possibly interest free) or through a computer-purchase program.

Personal/Family Life

Many events in an employee's life, although nonwork-related, affect an individual's work focus and ability to perform well. To address this to the mutual benefit of employer and employee, companies are putting modern management thinking into high gear through humanistic lifestyle-management programs and related employee, family, and domestic partner services.

Employee Assistance Programs

Employers are becoming more aware of how personal problems influence performance on the job, and many are offering employee assistance programs (EAPs) to help employees deal with personal issues. Employee assistance programs and/or referrals to community resources also often support the employee's family.

EAP components frequently embody wellness, drug and substance abuse counseling, and crisis intervention, utilizing either in-house or external vendors. The information you gather on this topic should touch on staff credentials, confidentiality pledge, and resource availability during night and weekend hours. In addition to expert advice, EAP representatives often distribute informational booklets or offer seminars on employee welfare topics.

Family and Dependent Care

Family and dependent care is a growing benefit area. With the increase in single-parent households and women working outside the home in many families today, the need for reliable child care is an issue of some magnitude for both employers and employees. Companies are becoming involved with family and dependent care in a number of different ways, recognizing that avoidable work interruptions and absences lead to lost productivity and burden the remaining workers, who must temporarily assume an additional workload.

Choices of child care resources and off-site providers are multifaceted and generally include nanny or au pair services, day-care centers, nursery schools, preferred in-home networks, and before- and after-school programs, along with special-needs assistance, referral programs, support groups, and community services. On-site or off-site, an organization may participate in a child-care consortium or network on behalf of employees. Screening criteria for evaluating venues and caregivers is extensive. At minimum, the checklist should include licensing and bonding, insurance, relevant training and experience, references, ratio of adults to children and ages of children supervised, development programs and behavioral rules, and hours of service. Some companies create a liaison with consulting services or provide referrals for child-care counseling regarding parenting issues, and others disseminate free publications on child-care education and parenting.

Cost savings may include access to company-sponsored day-care centers or programs or corporate purchasing discounts. Some organizations provide child-care expense reimbursement (particularly to accommodate an employee's extended work hours on weekends and in peak times), the routine need for sick-child care arrangements, and child care while traveling. Employers may help out directly or indirectly with holiday and summer camps for workers' children and emergency backup for sick-child care and off-hour baby-sitting. Child-care assistance can even go so far as to cover diaper service!

While certain employers provide financial subsidies or vouchers for child care, or vendor-purchased day-care slots at reduced rates, others grant flex-spending credits. Of note, *dependent care spending accounts* (DCSAs) are an important tax vehicle for managing child-care costs. See the "Health-Care Insurance" section in chapter 11 for more information on flexible spending accounts.

Elder care is also of growing importance to workers, and companies are receptive to the need for supportive counseling and referrals, as well as advice on a range of senior-citizen services—senior centers; adult day and personal care; assistance with daily living activities such as eating, bathing, and dressing; respite care; and transportation. Companies may also provide resource information on housing options, case management, in-home and intermediate care, and planning for assisted-care facility and nursing-home living alternatives.

Tuned-in employers may offer other family services, such as adoption assistance, information on schools for those with disabilities, special-needs support, counseling on student education achievement, and guidance in selecting and working with schools.

Financial and Legal Assistance
In another effort to assist their workforce, some companies have put in place financial and legal programs for dealing with various life events.

Financial education usually touches on money management and tax and life-stage personal financial planning. Topics include investment education, preparation for major purchases, debt management, college expense budgeting, retirement counseling, and estate planning. Some programs offer tax-preparation assistance and audit support.

Loan programs—for example, mortgage and education loans—and credit union memberships help workers manage their finances cost-effectively, frequently with the convenience of payroll deductions. Employers may offer loans under favorable conditions; for example, low-interest, no-interest, or below-market loans or bridge loans, unsecured by a mortgage.

Housing assistance primarily supports relocation, but some programs and services may also be available to all employees, such as assistance with down payment, security deposit, and the purchase process. Employing organizations may help with meeting loan preconditions and fee refunds, down payment and/or loan guarantees, and mortgage interest aid and mortgage buy-down points; or provide support in the form of grants for down payments. On occasion, organizations participate in building, owning, or subsidizing housing or housing developments, as well as home financing and refinancing.

Some companies also facilitate access to resources for personal legal matters. The type of legal plan will determine whether a prepayment for consultation is required or a fee for service (usually discounted) is arranged. Legal maintenance organizations (LMOs) are prepaid legal benefit plans. For a flat monthly fee, the participant has access to the services of a network of lawyers for handling such matters as real estate closings; costs incurred in marriage, divorce, and adoption; and drawing up wills. Other plans provide coverage on an ad hoc basis, may be either open or closed to employee choice of attorneys, and can be set up for either incurred expense reimbursement or direct supplier payment. You should check the qualifications of network legal providers; most attorneys are open to discussing relevant experience, American Bar Association standing, and malpractice insurance.

Group Buying Power

Group automobile, homeowners, marine, and mortgage insurance may be available at advantageous rates through some employers. Group purchasing power may extend to computers and peripheral equipment, such as printers, duplicating and fax machines, scanners, calculators, and so on. Responsibilities and expectations need to be expressly understood. It is quite common for businesses to offer employee discounts on company products, and sometimes companies also arrange for external discounted purchasing programs.

Volunteerism Support

Many employers encourage good-citizen community involvement on the part of employees, both directly and indirectly. Policy varies by employer and may involve both time and financial and service resources for programs, such as matching-grant or gift programs, support for volunteer activities, and payment of civic organization dues.

Compensation available to employees may include social responsibility pay, court duty pay, and military reserve training allowances, as well as charity, civic, and cultural events subsidies. On a related note, many companies participate in local recycling and energy-conservation efforts, both as a matter of practicality and as evidence of good citizenship.

HOW DOES BALANCING WORK AND PERSONAL LIFE AFFECT YOU?

Workers place a high value on quality of life and meeting personal needs, as well as monetary recognition for work well done. Quality of life often rests on a delicate balance of work, growth, training and development, as well as personal and family time, and community involvement. The emphasis will vary from one individual to another and over time, but all are important to a rewarding and satisfying lifestyle.

Flexible work arrangements, supplemental vacation time, and extension of benefits to family members are just some of the possibilities for negotiation. Know the company's policies and standard benefits package ahead of time. Read the benefits handbook and be prepared with questions. What is the company policy surrounding quality-of-life issues? Can you negotiate extra paid time off—vacation or personal time? How is service credit, often the basis for paid time off and other benefits, calculated? Are additional vacation days granted for superior individual or organizational performance? Does the company shut down, and when? Is there a probationary period for certain benefits for newly hired employees? Be aware that some benefits may have a tax impact. Ascertain what tax obligations, if any, unusual or unfamiliar benefits may carry; or check with an accountant.

If a flexible schedule is a high priority, develop a written proposal after initial interviews. After you start the job, review the arrangement with your management often. In negotiating for an alternative work arrangement or other benefit, make the business case that the accommodation will enhance your productivity—and deliver! Emphasize your strong commitment and unique individual value to the organization. Anticipate and prepare in advance to address any problems your work schedule might cause with co-workers or customers. Sometimes a trial period is established, so that both management and the employee can test the waters.

FROM THE EMPLOYER'S SIDE OF THE TABLE

Work arrangements, learning, and personal/family life programs are somewhat less heavily regulated than other benefits and thus are rich in opportunity for negotiation flexibility. Hiring managers should understand and be able to communicate the financial value of the standard benefits that the company offers, often equating to one-quarter to one-third of an employee's annual salary. Going one step further, enlightened employers, attuned to workers' changing needs and intent on managing barriers to doing the job, are actively focusing on making the workplace a place workers like to be.

In the past, employers sometimes interpreted an employee's commitment to family as diluting their commitment to work, often erroneously. But work and family are overlapping; and today there is seldom one person who is routinely at home to keep things going. Conventional work schedules and policies are no longer always viable. And replacing dissatisfied employees who terminate is a business drain; recruiting, training, and productivity losses caused by employee separations are costly. When considering the full spectrum of lost production, administrative compensation, recruiting expenses, the hiring manager's time, the new hire's learning curve, as well as benefits and severance assessments, estimates of turnover costs can range along a continuum, approaching 100 percent or more of a highly skilled former employee's *annual* salary.

Factors contributing to turnover are not limited to discontent with compensation levels or opportunity. Job satisfaction is a function of both organizational and job conditions; exit interviews reveal that departing employees are often concerned with lack of recognition, limited authority or autonomy, and work conflicts, either on the job or in the home. In reviewing working arrangements, learning aspirations, and personal/family values, keep in mind that there is no broad-brush, one-size-fits-all solution to worker needs. Doing what makes sense is common sense; providing equitable alternatives is a business plus and a positive motivator for employees.

Alternative staffing allows for creative, nontraditional employment schedules to everyone's advantage. Such staffing programs can enhance customer service by making feasible longer business hours and coverage of the company's noncore or nonpeak hours, maximizing the use of workspace and costly equipment, allowing workers to be more work-focused rather than time-conscious, and reducing the expense of turnover by aiding in worker retention.

Telecommuting is becoming a highly *possible* way of managing some work. Improved technology facilitates information sharing, reducing the need for large, centralized worker locations. The virtual office concept conserves facility space and aids obligations of large employers for Clean Air Act compliance but may require some technology or equipment to be placed in the employee's home and provisions made for its maintenance and repair, as well as utilities and supplies. In addition to production and quality control, employer interests include company liability, workers' compensation and safety issues, appropriate dependent care, availability of a separate work area in the home, and monitoring of FLSA and required overtime compliance. A review for adequate property and general liability insurance and zoning and local regulations may also be in order.

Some managers are challenged by work-at-home arrangements, fearing loss of control and lack of worker accountability. Regular feedback and periodic reassessment go a long way in alleviating these concerns. Both parties will benefit from frequent scheduled meetings to review assignments and performance, reaffirm the work relationship and company connection, and ensure ongoing communication.

Time off with pay is a high-expense benefit. Most plans are constructed around vacation allotment and a core group of holidays, with floating holidays building in long weekends or additional days off throughout the year. Vacation and personal time off helps workers reconcile the competing demands of work and personal life. Sometimes additional time off is a reasonable trade-off for employees who consistently work "above and beyond." Negotiate employee eligibility for enhanced vacation or nontraditional time off.

Micromanaging employees' time can send negative messages. Although it operates differently in different companies, flextime helps deal with paid time off and attendance issues by making employees more responsible for managing their own time. Some organizations allow workers to make up personal time taken during the day by extending the hours worked. Others allow employees to select a start and stop time within certain arrival and departure parameters, with required coverage of core work hours. In managing time off, consider the impact on operations and productivity. Operational efficiencies can be achieved through the use of flextime in organizations where special staffing requirements exist, for example, evening or weekend coverage. Rules for notification and scheduling of time off are key to effective utilization of flextime programs.

Pay for unused vacation and sick time may be an option; however, such cash-out plans can be managerially cumbersome and can increase the employer's administrative costs. It's often better to limit carryover to a maximum number of days and a specified time period, with employees forfeiting additional time not used within that period.

Employees spend long hours at the workplace and thrive in settings that are engineered to make their work safe, comfortable, and efficient. Applicable federal regulations like those of the Occupational Safety and Health Act of 1970 (OSHA), the Vocational Rehabilitation Act of 1973 (VRA), and the Americans with Disabilities Act of 1990 (ADA) govern the approach required for worker safety and disability accommodation.

In addition to the furniture and equipment required to do the work of the organization, the work atmosphere is telegraphed by company practices around formal or informal dress, smoking prohibitions, and programs that foster interaction with other employees.

Fitting in meals is a big part of today's longer work days. Management practices such as underwriting business luncheon conferences and scheduling team-building lunches serve to increase staff morale, as well as recognize the work being performed. Some employers even arrange dinner for their employees to encourage them to work late! In the same vein, convenient and adequately protected parking supports workers who are spending long days (and sometimes nights) on the job.

A company that supports employee development and lifelong learning is almost always more attractive to potential employees than one that does not. Education generates good will and trust, and it is the foundation of employee career development and upward mobility. One less expensive alternative to traditional classroom education is distance learning, in which employees take courses online or via televised lectures. Care must be taken that courses are properly accredited for transfer purposes. Development is a recruiting tool as well as a reward for veteran employees, appealing to workers who are interested in earning professional recognition and obtaining further education, usually job related. Time and cost must be carefully evaluated relative to the win-win advantages of investing in a highly skilled, competitive workforce. In recognition of the employer's investment, a piggyback condition for an education or development financial benefit might be the stipulation that an employee who leaves the company within a specified period of time after completing training must reimburse the company for the support received.

Troubled employees, under significant stress, often experience increased occurrences of absence, illness, and loss of productivity. Health-care consumption is costly. Employee assistance programs recognize and help mitigate the negative effects of a worker's personal health or job-performance problems.

Family-centered programs, such as dependent care, help meet the needs of single parents, two-income households, and workers in nontraditional living situations. Aware of the management and administrative investment and liability risks, some employers prefer to utilize third-party vendors or provide referrals to assist employees with meeting the need for dependent care.

The more sophisticated and self-responsible workforce of today profits from the availability of credentialed financial and legal resources. With the introduction of employee-guided investing of retirement savings, the need for practical education about investment concepts has been newly highlighted.

Many companies support worker volunteerism. Permitting employees to make a contribution to their community, while at the same time remaining productive, represents good corporate citizenship on the part of the employer as well.

All of the foregoing aspects of the worker's "hidden paycheck" offer valuable wiggle room for fitting the conditions of work to both the company's and the individual's ideals. Employee education about the value of such benefits, the linking of preferred flexible arrangements to performance, and "communication, communication, communication" will advance mutual understanding and appreciation of the reciprocal nature of flexible arrangements and ongoing adaptation of working conditions.

POINTS TO REMEMBER

+ Working conditions are highly negotiable.

+ Employees are placing greater emphasis on balancing work and personal life. Flexible work schedules are an effort toward achieving that balance.

+ Paid time off includes vacation days, holidays, personal days, and breaks.

+ Work atmosphere can impact an employee's productivity.

+ Learning is a lifelong process, integral to maintaining employability. Companies can support learning through work-related training, association memberships, and tuition reimbursement.

+ Companies may offer employee assistance programs to help workers with abuse counseling, crisis intervention, and wellness.

+ To support employees and minimize absence, companies are providing assistance with child care and elder care.

+ Various forms of legal and financial assistance are offered through some employers.

+ Business is recognizing the desirability of greater accommodation to the individual needs of workers.

+ The right mix of work, learning, and personal/family/community involvement changes over the life span of an individual.

WORK, LEARNING, AND LIFESTYLE PROGRAMS WORKSHEET

Many elements combine to make up the best conditions at work for the individual. Use the following worksheet to think through the many aspects of work arrangements, learning, and personal/family life influenced by the employment environment. Determine as your priorities those features that are most desirable for your own situation and prepare for negotiation on these issues. Be clear on any tax advantages or obligations arising from a particular arrangement.

BENEFIT FEATURE	PRIORITY ITEM (✔)	RELATIVE POWER/ OPTIONS	EMPLOYER FLEXIBILITY	NOTES
Work and schedule flexibility				
Work location/ telecommuting				
Paid time off				
Unpaid time off				
Work environment, socialization, safety, and convenience services				
Meals				

continues

continued

BENEFIT FEATURE	PRIORITY ITEM (✔)	RELATIVE POWER/ OPTIONS	EMPLOYER FLEXIBILITY	NOTES
Parking				
Education and development				
Lifestyle management and employee assistance				
Family and dependent care				
Other family services				

BENEFIT FEATURE	PRIORITY ITEM (✔)	RELATIVE POWER/ OPTIONS	EMPLOYER FLEXIBILITY	NOTES
Financial and legal assistance				
Loan programs and housing assistance				
Group purchasing arrangements				
Product and buying discounts				
Community involvement/ volunteerism				

BUSINESS ENTERTAINMENT, TRAVEL, AND EXPENSE REIMBURSEMENT POLICIES

Whether and how employees will be expected to entertain for business purposes may be open for discussion. Many jobs require travel, the conditions and comfort of which can differ depending on how much of its funds the company allows you to spend. The extension of company entertainment and travel resources for personal use is a negotiable perquisite.

Entertainment and travel on behalf of a business are commonly employer-absorbed expenses. Business entertainment, often both a productive and an enjoyable aspect of work, has come under heightened scrutiny in recent years by both the government and management in tax-compliance and cost-containment efforts. Many companies are viewing entertainment and some travel expenses as areas in which they can make cutbacks.

WHAT ARE BUSINESS ENTERTAINMENT, TRAVEL, AND EXPENSE REIMBURSEMENT POLICIES ALL ABOUT?

Entertainment

Some entertainment perks serve the dual purpose of rewarding employees and facilitating business contacts. For example, sports and theater tickets may be made available through the employer at no charge or at special discounts. Historically, senior executives often enjoyed memberships to prestige clubs, such as country clubs, athletic clubs, or tennis clubs, with the employer assuming payment of initiation fees, annual dues, and assessments. Today, however, the tax ramifications of such arrangements require more elaborate and extensive accounting and reporting, and employer-sponsored memberships have lost momentum.

Business entertainment at home, once very common, seems to be less so today. Some employers encourage the use of employer-owned or employer-leased facilities for business entertainment.

Travel

Business travel is an accepted part of many jobs. Spouse accompaniment on trips may also be supportable in a variety of circumstances, as well as travel-necessitated dependent care and even pet-care expenses. Some business travel can successfully combine business and pleasure. Encouraging family members to accompany employees (even at the individual's expense) to a business meeting, promotion, seminar, or convention held, for example, at a luxury resort can be a valued acknowledgement of the work-family connection.

Sometimes an employer pays for travel directly through accounts with a travel agency. Air, rail, and bus, as well as destination car rental and taxi expenses are usually reimbursable, along with terminal and local parking, luggage handling, and tips.

Employees who are frequent travelers may be eligible for airline and hotel clubs, as well as frequent-flyer miles and guest credits. Air travel guidelines regarding class of travel or seating and mileage credits vary.

Reimbursement for automobile travel, either by company car, rental car, or personal vehicle, is prevalent. Most often, an automobile allowance is established for gas, maintenance, and insurance. Purchase or lease of an automobile may be possible; make, model, equipment such as a car phone or pager, upkeep, and turnover timeframes are defined more often than not, but may be negotiable. Most companies have car leasing and rental standards that guide the aspects of rental agreements, for example, whether and what level of rental insurance coverage is required.

Access to the company fleet or assignment of a company car will eliminate the need for reimbursement, except for out-of-pocket gasoline charges and related travel expenses, such as tolls. In some arrangements, an employee may be allowed to use a company car for both business and personal reasons. In such cases, the employee will likely face certain tax obligations.

Additional travel-related reimbursable items generally include parking, travel-appended taxes and fees, laundry and dry cleaning, and miscellaneous expenses while on the road, such as meeting rooms, office support, photocopying and faxing, and other administrative necessities. In the case of travel outside the United States, a visa, a passport, and any required immunizations may be covered.

Meals

When an employee travels on behalf of the company, it is customary for the business to reimburse the cost of meals. Some organizations have meal expense guidelines; others expect employees to use their judgment, as costs are impacted by event and locale. In some cases, breakfast and dinner are covered, but lunch is at the employee's expense, as it customarily is during nontravel work time. Covered meal expenses may or may not include alcohol and expensing of fellow employees' meals.

Accommodations

Choice of hotel facilities and accommodations may be limited by certain criteria or restricted to preferred vendors. In lieu of obligation for the expense of a hotel, an employee staying with friends or family who live in the area may be permitted to purchase a gift at company expense for the host or hostess.

Commuting

Many large organizations actively support alternative transportation to work through commuter van pools and public-transportation subsidies. Some employers encourage ride-share arrangements by purchasing and operating van transportation for workers who live in areas without convenient public transportation or by subsidizing employees who form and use car pools.

HOW DO BUSINESS ENTERTAINMENT, TRAVEL, AND EXPENSE REIMBURSEMENT POLICIES AFFECT YOU?

The usual manner of paying for employee-incurred business expenses is through a combination of advance cash funds and reimbursement of expenses based on credit card charges or cash receipts. Alternative practice also includes per diem (daily) allowance payments instead of reimbursement of actual and billed expenses.

If the job will require travel or encompass business entertainment, find out the company's expectations and reimbursement norms during your discussions with the employer. Explore whether a corporate credit card, exclusively for business travel and entertainment, would be practical, and whether a telephone credit card will be supplied for use during periods of business travel.

Be sure to know the prospective employer's reimbursement policies. Once on the job, obtain and save necessary receipts and documentation of expenditures, including those for incidental expenses and business-necessitated home entertainment. Logs, diaries, receipts, and other records are generally required to substantiate expenses and obtain reimbursement. Notes should clearly detail the business reason for the expense.

FROM THE EMPLOYER'S SIDE OF THE TABLE

Review your company's guidelines for business entertainment and travel with a recruit during the hiring discussion. Having an established policy on expense reimbursement creates a favorable impression of the company's way of doing business.

While business travel and entertainment are not benefits per se, they are influential aspects of some jobs and work environments. Company policies in this area may affect an employee's successful management of travel and entertainment-related job responsibilities. In this light, it makes sense to arrange for fair and equitable reimbursement of reasonable expenses incurred by employees as representatives of the business. Solid accounting advice will ensure that an organization's expense reimbursement practices are cognizant of tax reporting requirements.

POINTS TO REMEMBER

- Entertainment expense is closely scrutinized by both the company and the government.

- Expenses that companies will reimburse may include business entertainment, car and air travel, accommodations, and meals.

- Companies may either pay direct or reimburse actual expenses or pay a daily expense allowance.

ENTERTAINMENT AND TRAVEL WORKSHEET

Use the following worksheet to plan your discussions about the employer's entertainment and travel expectations and reimbursement policies during the negotiation. Be aware of the tax aspects of different arrangements.

BENEFIT FEATURE	PRIORITY ITEM (✓)	RELATIVE POWER/ OPTIONS	EMPLOYER FLEXIBILITY	NOTES
Business entertainment policy and customs				
Company car				
Modes of business travel/travel comfort and convenience				
Meals				

BENEFIT FEATURE	PRIORITY ITEM (✔)	RELATIVE POWER/ OPTIONS	EMPLOYER FLEXIBILITY	NOTES
Accommodations				
Reimbursement methods				
Other entertainment and travel expenses				

EXECUTIVE AND SUPPLEMENTAL BENEFITS

Executive privileges and supplemental benefits are fertile ground for negotiating a job offer. Because these areas are often nonstandard, employers may be better able to make concessions and tailor job benefits to the needs of the individual. Most employees are not eligible for executive-level benefits; however, being acquainted with some of the provisions made for senior people may help in formulating job-offer negotiations for unique individual situations.

Executive perquisites by definition do not extend to all or most of the population; rather, they apply only to senior management. While many of the individual perquisites are not necessarily exclusive to the executive population, in combination they may represent a dollar amount equivalent that only senior management contributions to the organization's bottom line can justify. Enhanced offers must be reviewed for their tax impact and affect, if any, on the Employee Retirement Income Security Act of 1974 (ERISA) and post-ERISA legislation compliance.

ERISA is comprehensive legislation that regulates certain private employer pension and welfare programs with regard to a number of plan aspects, notably participation exclusivity, vesting, fiduciary responsibility, funding, and plan termination. ERISA encourages employers to meet its requirements by providing business tax advantages for compliance. Because enhanced offers often cover extraordinary benefits that could place compliance at risk, employers must manage executive benefits with ERISA provisions in mind.

WHAT ARE EXECUTIVE AND SUPPLEMENTAL BENEFITS ALL ABOUT?

Executive benefits can run the gamut from a cash offset for lost pension benefits from a former position to extended medical and disability coverage and special claims processing, enhanced life insurance, supplemental retirement, ERISA excess and supplemental savings plans in the form of deferred compensation, and reimbursement for the costs of benefits and legal fees. Much of executive compensation is structured as long-term incentive awards—capital, often deferred, and equity (stock or securities) ownership—that vest over time. Deferred compensation—all or a portion of base salary, bonus, or long-term incentive—may be elective or mandatory, paid in cash, stock or securities, or life insurance. The return and timing of payment is plan–specific. Some organizations have holding stipulations, requiring executives to retain company stock at a certain number of shares or value for a period of years.

The goal of these long-term incentive plans is to align stakeholder—shareholder, company, and executive—interests, emphasizing longer-term performance and commitment to the organization. Clarity about performance measurement is extremely important to all parties.

The variations on long-term cash and equity incentive vehicles are many. Long term incentive (LTI) plans may be qualified (meeting certain criteria and carrying tax advantages) or nonqualified (more flexible, but somewhat more at risk). LTI plans may be either performance- or market-based and payouts may be in cash, stock, or a combination of cash and stock.

Capital plans include performance units, profit and gainsharing programs, and annuity supplements. With performance unit plans (PUPs), a block of units is assigned to the executive at the start of a specified performance period. Each unit represents a fixed value. Payout (in cash and/or stock) is contingent on a formula for performance, usually a financial result, relative to preset goals. Among the many other forms of performance- and market-based plans are book units, dividend equivalents (equivalent to the dividend per share of stock), phantom stock, and stock appreciation rights (SARs).

Stock grant plans can take the form of stock appreciation or full-value grants. In performance share plans (PSPs), stock shares or units are awarded contingent upon achievement of predetermined performance goals.

Incentive stock option (ISO) plans are by far the most prevalent equity program. Discount stock options are options to purchase shares at less than a stock's fair market value on the grant date. Other option plans are premium options, where the purchase price is set above fair market value on the date of grant; and indexed options, with value tied to a specific index or formula.

Stock may be restricted, subject to a period of limitations and conditional forfeiture prior to vesting; or unrestricted, granted free and clear of conditions. Shares and options can, of course, increase or decrease in worth.

The formula for long-term incentives at target performance is frequently a percentage of the employee's salary or a target percent of the salary range midpoint geared to the employee's level in the organization. Performance time periods may be based on a rolling schedule, so that a payout occurs annually for the most mature cycle, usually a three- to five-year performance period.

Nonqualified deferred compensation plans (NQDCs) often mirror 401(k) or similar plans for those highly compensated employees whose investment in a 401(k) is limited by ERISA restrictions. The employee can accumulate capital by postponing receipt of a portion of earned compensation, or company contributions can fund the plan. Vesting may be incremental, with an eye toward retention of key talent. (Funds are held in trust, but employer contributions may be vulnerable in cases of severe business reversal.)

Supplemental executive retirement plans (SERPs) provide higher benefit levels than qualified plans and may recognize prior service or restore an early retirement pension reduction. SERPs are typically unsecured obligations. Payment guarantees may be insured through various vehicles, for example: rabbi trusts, other trust and insurance arrangements and corporate-owned life insurance, surety bonds, or annuities. (A rabbi trust is an irrevocable trust established to secure employer promises to pay deferred compensation; in the event of bankruptcy, the trust is endangered. A secular trust is somewhat similar to a rabbi trust in that it is designed to protect retirement or deferred compensation; however, its assets are protected from general creditor bankruptcy claims.)

Travel perquisites can encompass an upgraded company car, limited or on-demand personal use of the company airplane, premium first- or business-class air travel and air club membership, a driver or chauffeured limousine, premium hotel accommodations, spousal accompaniment on trips, and even reimbursement for elder, child, and pet care expenses. Other perks include special parking, special dining, an apartment in the city or use of upscale company-owned housing, and preferred entertainment privileges. Country club and other club memberships, popular in the past, have declined as a result of changed tax implications.

Many executive perks provide psychic, as well as financial, income. Opportunity for prestigious board memberships at other organizations and for consulting fees may also exist for senior management. Membership in an elite business fraternity, high visibility through corporate responsibility initiatives, and public recognition for leadership all contribute to the perception of work-related quality of life.

Enhanced "getting settled" relocation packages may cover new furnishings and unusual expenses, for example, transportation and storage of boats. Various perks can involve savings on vacation homes, domestic help, a home security system, and telephone and credit cards. Convenience services may be available, such as concierge assistance for ordering flowers, dry cleaning, and automobile maintenance; home maintenance help; and home and personal security services. Amenities can even include stress-reducing or therapeutic massage.

Supplemental medical and dental benefits may feature waiver of insurance waiting periods and/or medical expense reimbursement. Employers may offer early retirement and postretirement special insurance coverage, such as employer-paid excess personal liability and life insurance, accidental death and dismemberment, dependent life insurance, and supplemental long-term insurance carried into retirement. Certain supplemental plans offer spousal inclusion in some or all of the executive's enhanced benefits. The nontraditional nature of their compensation makes financial planning and counseling, investment planning, retirement and estate planning, and tax planning and preparation particularly valuable to executives.

HOW DO EXECUTIVE AND SUPPLEMENTAL BENEFITS AFFECT YOU?

Most executive employment packages are documented carefully, often as part of an employment contract. These contracts may or may not be structured as automatically renewable.

It is also important to document the settlement of executive and supplemental benefits in the event of separation, whether voluntary or involuntary. In takeover situations, agreement provisions may trigger "golden parachutes," which are, essentially, enhanced severance arrangements and may provide for accelerated vesting or payout of deferred incentive compensation.

Long-term incentives may be prorated or paid out early, unreduced. The phrase "golden handcuffs" sometimes refers to long-term incentives that pay out only if the individual is actively employed by the organization for a given period of time.

Tax advice is critical in crafting the most advantageous collection of supplemental benefits. Supplemental benefits may be considered taxable income for both executive and nonexecutive employees, unless they are "de minimis"—without substantial material value, per a given amount. The future value of indirect or equity ownership is determined by probability costing, because the value cannot be directly determined. A newer tax-planning device is transferable stock options, in which the financial benefit to the executive is structured advantageously relative to estate taxes.

FROM THE EMPLOYER'S SIDE OF THE TABLE

Many executive benefits are exclusive to key members of the management team, whose leadership most directly impacts the achievement of organizational goals. The governing precept for executive compensation and long-term incentive plans is that they be closely subject to the company's overall business strategy. Criteria for performance measurement and rules for quantification of expected business results must be clearly communicated. Reward formulas should significantly differentiate short- and long-term award levels for baseline (threshold), target, and maximum performance.

The executive compensation arena is extremely complex. Much of supplemental benefit plan tax, accounting, and disclosure and reporting is regulated at the federal level through the Internal Revenue Service (IRS) and the Securities and Exchange Commission (SEC), and governed by the Financial Accounting Standards Board (FASB). Review all proposals for extraordinary compensation and benefits carefully with your legal, tax, and accounting resources.

Deferred income is very characteristic of executive compensation. To be appealing to the executive, voluntary deferral arrangements must attend to executive tax concerns. In general, currently, if the executive can obtain the money, it is considered taxable (constructive receipt). If the company defers income on behalf of the executive, the deferred funds cannot be used by the executive as collateral (economic benefit).

Use good judgment in crafting and substantiating executive and supplemental benefits offers. Increasing publicity and media attention to lucrative executive compensation arrangements have reduced shareholder (and worker) tolerance and contributed to a negative public perception of executive compensation. Eventually, public opinion may act to curb disproportionate compensation and unfounded special treatment for executives.

POINTS TO REMEMBER

* It is common for companies to recognize the significant contributions of senior executives to the bottom line through supplemental benefits.

* Supplemental benefit areas are highly negotiable.

* Federal and state income tax considerations are a big factor in structuring advantageous executive and unique supplemental-benefits packages.

* Seek the advice of legal and tax professionals in structuring supplemental benefit provisions.

* All supplemental benefits agreements should be carefully and fully documented in the employment contract.

* Even if you are not eligible for executive benefits, familiarity with them can help you formulate negotiations for unique situations.

* Much of executive compensation is long-term, to encourage commitment to the organization.

* Executives may qualify for enhanced health and life insurance, travel and relocation packages, and a multitude of other perks.

EXECUTIVE AND SUPPLEMENTAL BENEFITS WORKSHEET

Use the following worksheet to think through any executive benefits that may be attainable through negotiation. Review executive incentive plan eligibility and vesting, funding, awards, performance and measurement criteria, payout frequency, and exercise rights and restrictions. Be sure to look at supplemental benefits from a tax perspective to gauge the true value of the enhancement.

BENEFIT FEATURE	PRIORITY ITEM (✔)	RELATIVE POWER/ OPTIONS	EMPLOYER FLEXIBILITY	NOTES
Enhanced offer				
Executive equity ownership plan				
Long-term capital				
Long-term equity				
Deferred compensation/SERP				

BENEFIT FEATURE	PRIORITY ITEM (✔)	RELATIVE POWER/ OPTIONS	EMPLOYER FLEXIBILITY	NOTES
Preferred travel				
Executive perks				
Supplemental insurance benefits				
Financial planning/ tax advice				

Compensation and Benefits Analysis Worksheet

The following worksheet encompasses all of the major aspects of compensation and benefits. You can use it to estimate and assess the total compensation package of your current or former position, as well as that of the new position you are being offered. Quantifying the variables in this way will help you decide which parts of the offer are financially acceptable, and which parts you will want to negotiate. You can also use the worksheet to evaluate one job offer against another.

Not all of the following benefits are linked in every instance to a direct financial reward, but they may add to the quality of work and/or personal life.

See parts IV and V for additional worksheets that enable you to do a more in-depth analysis and prioritization of many of the following variables.

Salary and Bonus

BENEFIT	DESCRIPTION	CURRENT OR MOST RECENT JOB: EMPLOYEE COST/ DOLLAR VALUE	PROPOSED JOB/ JOB OFFER #1: EMPLOYEE COST/ DOLLAR VALUE	JOB OFFER #2: EMPLOYEE COST/ DOLLAR VALUE
Base salary/wages				
Short-term incentives				
Long-term incentives				
Equity ownership				

Health Care

BENEFIT	DESCRIPTION	CURRENT OR MOST RECENT JOB: EMPLOYEE COST/ DOLLAR VALUE	PROPOSED JOB/ JOB OFFER #1: EMPLOYEE COST/ DOLLAR VALUE	JOB OFFER #2: EMPLOYEE COST/ DOLLAR VALUE
Medical insurance				
Dental/other insurance				
Prescription drug coverage				
Health-care spending account				
Wellness programs				

Income Protection

BENEFIT	DESCRIPTION	CURRENT OR MOST RECENT JOB: EMPLOYEE COST/ DOLLAR VALUE	PROPOSED JOB/ JOB OFFER #1: EMPLOYEE COST/ DOLLAR VALUE	JOB OFFER #2: EMPLOYEE COST/ DOLLAR VALUE
Sick pay				
Short-term disability				
Long-term disability				
Long-term-care insurance				

BENEFIT	DESCRIPTION	CURRENT OR MOST RECENT JOB: EMPLOYEE COST/ DOLLAR VALUE	PROPOSED JOB/ JOB OFFER #1: EMPLOYEE COST/ DOLLAR VALUE	JOB OFFER #2: EMPLOYEE COST/ DOLLAR VALUE
Life insurance				
Extended/other financial insurance coverage				
Business liability insurance				

Retirement

BENEFIT	DESCRIPTION	CURRENT OR MOST RECENT JOB: EMPLOYEE COST/ DOLLAR VALUE	PROPOSED JOB/ JOB OFFER #1: EMPLOYEE COST/ DOLLAR VALUE	JOB OFFER #2: EMPLOYEE COST/ DOLLAR VALUE
Defined-benefit pension plan				
Defined-contribution plan				
Stock/stock options				
Portability of retirement funds				

Involuntary Termination

BENEFIT	DESCRIPTION	CURRENT OR MOST RECENT JOB: EMPLOYEE COST/ DOLLAR VALUE	PROPOSED JOB/ JOB OFFER #1: EMPLOYEE COST/ DOLLAR VALUE	JOB OFFER #2: EMPLOYEE COST/ DOLLAR VALUE
Involuntary separation package				
Benefits continuation/ payouts				
Outplacement services				

Relocation

BENEFIT	DESCRIPTION	CURRENT OR MOST RECENT JOB: EMPLOYEE COST/ DOLLAR VALUE	PROPOSED JOB/ JOB OFFER #1: EMPLOYEE COST/ DOLLAR VALUE	JOB OFFER #2: EMPLOYEE COST/ DOLLAR VALUE
Lump-sum expense offset				
Assistance with sale of existing home				
House-hunting allowance				

BENEFIT	DESCRIPTION	CURRENT OR MOST RECENT JOB: EMPLOYEE COST/ DOLLAR VALUE	PROPOSED JOB/ JOB OFFER #1: EMPLOYEE COST/ DOLLAR VALUE	JOB OFFER #2: EMPLOYEE COST/ DOLLAR VALUE
Moving expenses				
New home purchase assistance				
Miscellaneous support				

Work/Life Balance

BENEFIT	DESCRIPTION	CURRENT OR MOST RECENT JOB: EMPLOYEE COST/ DOLLAR VALUE	PROPOSED JOB/ JOB OFFER #1: EMPLOYEE COST/ DOLLAR VALUE	JOB OFFER #2: EMPLOYEE COST/ DOLLAR VALUE
Schedule and location flexibility				
Paid time off				
Time off without pay				
Work environment				

BENEFIT	DESCRIPTION	CURRENT OR MOST RECENT JOB: EMPLOYEE COST/ DOLLAR VALUE	PROPOSED JOB/ JOB OFFER #1: EMPLOYEE COST/ DOLLAR VALUE	JOB OFFER #2: EMPLOYEE COST/ DOLLAR VALUE
Meals				
Parking				
Commuter assistance				
Career development and education reimbursement				

continues

Work/Life Balance, continued

BENEFIT	DESCRIPTION	CURRENT OR MOST RECENT JOB: EMPLOYEE COST/ DOLLAR VALUE	PROPOSED JOB/ JOB OFFER #1: EMPLOYEE COST/ DOLLAR VALUE	JOB OFFER #2: EMPLOYEE COST/ DOLLAR VALUE
Lifestyle management and employee assistance				
Family and dependent care support				
Other family services				

BENEFIT	DESCRIPTION	CURRENT OR MOST RECENT JOB: EMPLOYEE COST/ DOLLAR VALUE	PROPOSED JOB/ JOB OFFER #1: EMPLOYEE COST/ DOLLAR VALUE	JOB OFFER #2: EMPLOYEE COST/ DOLLAR VALUE
Loan programs and housing assistance				
Financial and legal assistance				
Group purchasing/ product discounts				
Volunteerism support				

Business Entertainment and Travel

BENEFIT	DESCRIPTION	CURRENT OR MOST RECENT JOB: EMPLOYEE COST/ DOLLAR VALUE	PROPOSED JOB/ JOB OFFER #1: EMPLOYEE COST/ DOLLAR VALUE	JOB OFFER #2: EMPLOYEE COST/ DOLLAR VALUE
Business entertainment reimbursement				
Company car				
Business travel expense reimbursement				
Other entertainment and travel benefits				

Executive and Supplemental Benefits

BENEFIT	DESCRIPTION	CURRENT OR MOST RECENT JOB: EMPLOYEE COST/ DOLLAR VALUE	PROPOSED JOB/ JOB OFFER #1: EMPLOYEE COST/ DOLLAR VALUE	JOB OFFER #2: EMPLOYEE COST/ DOLLAR VALUE
Enhanced offer packages				
Executive equity ownership plan				
Long-term cash				
Long-term equity				

continues

Executive and Supplemental Benefits, continued

BENEFIT	DESCRIPTION	CURRENT OR MOST RECENT JOB: EMPLOYEE COST/ DOLLAR VALUE	PROPOSED JOB/ JOB OFFER #1: EMPLOYEE COST/ DOLLAR VALUE	JOB OFFER #2: EMPLOYEE COST/ DOLLAR VALUE
Deferred compensation/SERP				
Supplemental insurance				
Executive perks/other				

Glossary of
Compensation and Benefits Terms

Reprinted from *ACA Glossary of Compensation and Benefits Terms,* © 1999 with permission from the American Compensation Association (ACA), 14040 N. Northsight Blvd., Scottsdale, AZ 85260, USA; telephone (602) 951-9191, fax (602) 483-8352.

401(k)   A defined-contribution benefit plan established by an employer. It enables the employee to make pretax contributions through salary-reduction agreements within the format of a cash or defined plan.

403(b)   A tax-sheltered annuity plan for nonprofit and public-sector organizations. There are similarities between 401(k) and 403(b) plans.

accidental death and dismemberment insurance (AD&D)   Insurance providing benefits in the event of loss of life, limbs, or eyesight as the result of an accident. It is a term insurance product sold on a cents-per-thousand basis.

annual bonus   Usually a lump-sum payment (cash, shares, etc.) made once a year in addition to an employee's normal salary or wage for a fiscal or calendar year. Generally nondiscretionary and not based on pre-determined performance criteria or standards (which distinguishes an annual bonus from an incentive).

annuity   Periodic payment made to a pensioner over a fixed period of time, or until his or her death. To purchase an annuity means to pay a lump sum or make periodic payments to an insurance company. In return, the insurance company guarantees that certain periodic payments will be made to the participant, as long as he or she lives beyond the first due date of the annuity.

area differential (1) Allowance paid to compensate expatriate employees for medium-term cultural and hardship factors present in his or her country of assignment compared to the base country. (2) Allowance paid to domestic or expatriate employees in certain geographic areas based on different average pay levels and/or cost of living.

automatic wage progression Automatically increasing wages after specified periods of service, until the employee reaches the top of his or her salary range. Automatic wage progression often is achieved through an automatic step-rate pay system. (Also known as *length-of-service increases.*)

base wage rate (or base rate) The hourly rate or salary paid for a job performed. Does not include shift differentials, benefits, overtime, incentive premiums, or any pay element other than the base rate.

bonus An after-the-fact discretionary reward or payment based on the performance of an individual, a group of workers operating as a unit, a division or business unit, or an entire workforce. Payments may be made in cash, shares, share options, or other items of value.

book unit award plan A type of long-term incentive plan in which an employee is awarded stock units valued at the book value per share. In a book-value appreciation plan, an increase in the book value of the stock accrues to the benefit of the employee. In a full-value book-value plan, the full value of the book value units accrues to the benefit of the employee, usually after fulfilling a vesting period. See *book value.*

book value (BV) The total shareholders' equity divided by the number of common shares outstanding. Book value is sometimes used in incentive plans in privately owned companies where a fair market value of shares is not readily known.

business travel accident insurance An insurance plan that provides benefits for an accident which occurs while an employee is traveling on company business.

cafeteria plan As defined in the Internal Revenue Code Section 125, a flexible benefits arrangement in which participants may choose between taxable and nontaxable compensation elements. Examples include premium conversion (pretax premium), flexible spending accounts, and broad employee-choice programs that include certain tax-advantaged features. See *flexible benefits.*

call-back pay A guarantee of pay for a minimum number of hours when employees are called back to their work at times when they are not scheduled to work. They receive pay for at least the minimum number of hours established even if they do not work that number of hours.

call-in pay Guaranteed pay for a set minimum amount of time for employees who report to work at the usual time and for whom there is no work. The employees receive pay for at least the specified minimum number of hours even if they did not work the minimum number of hours. Sometimes called *report-in pay.*

cash balance pension plan A defined benefit plan that looks like a defined contribution plan. Features include annual or monthly account additions made at a specified rate (e.g., five percent of pay) and that grow at a stated rate (e.g., one-year T-bill rate in effect on the first day of the plan year).

coinsurance The percent of covered expense paid by the covered individual versus the percent paid by the benefit plan (e.g., the plan pays 80 percent coinsurance for hospital expenses, and the employee pays 20 percent coinsurance).

commission A predetermined, direct cash payment made as incentive pay for the sale of a product or service, usually calculated as a percentage of the gross sale amount or flat amount for each unit sold. A commission-only compensation program is sometimes known as *full commission* or *straight commission.*

compensation strategy/philosophy/policy The principles that guide design, implementation, and administration of a compensation program at an organization. The strategy ensures that a compensation program, consisting of both pay and benefits, supports an organization's mission, goals, and business objectives. It may also specify what programs will be used and how they will be administered. The philosophy ensures that a compensation program supports an organization's culture. The policy ensures that a compensation program carries out the compensation strategy while supporting the compensation philosophy.

comprehensive health plan   A medical insurance program that provides for coverage of almost all medical expenses under one plan or contract. Before benefits are payable, the plan usually requires an employee to pay an annual deductible and then coinsurance (usually 20 percent) thereafter until an annual out-of-pocket maximum is met. After the maximum is met, the plan provides 100 percent coinsurance for the rest of the year.

contributory benefit plan   A program in which the employee contributes part (or all) of the cost, and any remainder is covered by the employer.

coordination of benefits (COB)   A group health insurance policy provision designed to prevent an employee from collecting more than 100 percent of the charges for the same medical expense when the employee or one of their dependents is covered by two medical plans (i.e., as an insured under one plan and as a dependent under another). Also referred to as *standard COB.*

corporate-owned life insurance (COLI)   Life-insurance policies that insure the lives of selected executive-level employees where the company is either owner and beneficiary, or ownership and beneficial interest is split with the executive. The organization pays the premiums, retains ownership of the insurance, and receives tax-free proceeds when the participants die. The amount of insurance purchased is calculated to recover the cost of executive benefits to be provided under a nonqualified plan. However, the death-benefit proceeds may be used by the organization for any purpose. See *split-dollar insurance.*

deductible   An amount paid by an employee for covered expenses in a group medical or dental plan before the plan pays benefits. A typical plan would follow a calendar year schedule, and specify an individual deductible (e.g., $250) and a higher family deductible (e.g., $500).

deferred compensation   Any of a number of compensation payments that are payable to an employee at some point in the future. These include voluntary or mandatory deferral of earned incentives, as well as earnings and retirement plan vehicles.

defined-benefit pension plan   Both the Employee Retirement Income Security Act of 1974 (ERISA) and the Internal Revenue Code (IRC) define any retirement plan that provides for future income and is not an individual account plan as a defined-benefit plan. It is a pension plan that specifies the benefits, or the methods of determining the benefits, but not the level or rate of contribution. Contributions are determined actuarially on the basis of the benefits expected to become payable.

defined-contribution pension plan (capital accumulation)   A defined-contribution or individual-account plan as defined by the Employee Retirement Income Security Act of 1974 (ERISA) and the Internal Revenue Code (IRC) as a plan that provides for future income from an individual account for each participant with benefits based solely on (1) the amount contributed to the participant's account, plus (2) any income, expenses, gains and losses, and forfeitures of accounts of other participants that may be allocated to the participant's account. The benefit amount to be received by the participant at retirement is unknown until retirement.

director and officer (D&O) liability insurance   Insurance to protect members of boards of directors and key officers against lawsuits for various types of malpractice or oversight.

discount stock option   Rights to a stock option at a price less than 100 percent of fair market value on the date of grant.

dividend equivalents   In some incentive plans, participants are paid an amount of money equal to the dividends that are paid per share of common stock.

employee assistance programs (EAPs)   Programs that provide counseling or referral services to employees. Services vary by employer, but include assistance with chemical dependency, and psychological, financial, legal, family, and career counseling. Services are usually provided by a third party to protect employee confidentiality, but may be provided internally by some employers. Generally, participation is voluntary unless a mandatory management referral is made.

employee benefits   A collection of noncash compensation elements including but not limited to income protection, health coverage, retirement savings, vacation, and income supplements for employees, provided in whole or in part by employer payments.

employee contributions   Payments made by an employee to fund a specific benefit, thereby defraying part or all of the employer's cost.

employee share-ownership plan (ESOP)   A plan that enables qualified employees to receive shares that they accrued as plan participants at no cost to themselves upon retirement or separation from the organization.

employment contract   A contract that provides an incoming employee with a written guarantee of receiving certain rewards, regardless of the results produced on the job. The employee also may agree not to (1) compete with the present employer for the duration of employment and some reasonable time period thereafter, (2) disclose or discuss secret formulas, etc., that are of value to the employer, and (3) hold another job.

executive benefits   Forms of noncash compensation provided to a small number of executives that are in excess of the benefits provided to all other employees (e.g., company car, supplemental insurance coverages, etc.).

exempt   A term referring to employees who are exempt from the overtime provisions of the U.S. Fair Labor Standards Act of 1938 (FLSA). These groups include executives, administrative employees, professional employees, and those engaged in outside sales as defined by the FLSA.

expatriate   An employee who is assigned temporarily (usually one to five years) outside his or her home or base country. Also referred to as *foreign service employee, international assignee,* or *international staff.*

extrinsic rewards   Work-related rewards received for performance that have value measurable in monetary or financial terms. The opposite is *intrinsic rewards,* which relates to personal satisfaction derived from performing a job well.

family leave   Time off, either paid or unpaid, provided for an employee to care for their own serious medical condition or a seriously ill family member, a new baby, or an adopted child. Family leave policies usually are broader than parental leave policies.

flat benefit retirement plan   A defined-benefit pension plan that provides benefits unrelated to earnings. An example would be a plan that specifies a certain amount of money per month, per year of service ($25 per month, per year of credited service).

flexible benefits   A plan under Internal Revenue Code Section 125 that permits employees to select cash and/or benefits they want from a menu of choices provided by the employer. In some plans, employees receive subsidies (credits) from the employer to help pay for their choices. Plans commonly include tax-advantaged features and allow employees to select between taxable and nontaxable forms of compensation. Also known as *cafeteria plans.*

flexible spending accounts   Under Internal Revenue Code Section 125, employees can set aside money on a pretax basis to pay for eligible unreimbursed health and dependent day care expenses on a tax-free basis. Accounts are subject to annual maximums and forfeiture rules.

flextime   A policy that allows employees to choose convenient starting and quitting times, and under some plans, an extended lunchtime, while still requiring the standard number of hours each day or week.

front-end bonus   A specific bonus given at the beginning of a service period, usually for accepting an employment offer. It could also be used at the beginning of a new reward program. Also called a *signing bonus,* it typically is used to offset forfeited benefits left behind in a previous situation.

gainsharing   Any one of a number of incentive programs (e.g., Rucker, Improshare, Scanlon) designed to share productivity gains with employees as a group.

gatekeeper   Usually a primary-care physician (i.e., family practice, pediatrician, gynecologist, internist) who is responsible for directing the medical care of an employee and covered dependents. To receive full benefits, employees and covered dependents must be referred to other medical specialists by their gatekeeper physician. This type of physician generally is found in HMOs and point-of-service health-care networks.

golden handcuffs   Employee benefits and/or payments or incentives linked to an individual's continued employment with an organization. Leaving the organization results in forfeiting the value.

golden parachute   An employment contract that provides for an increase or acceleration of payments or vesting or other rights such as additional payments for the employee, upon change of control of the corporation as defined in the contract, or upon change of control coupled with a change in the employee's job or status.

group universal life plan (GULP)   A form of group life insurance that combines term protection with an investment element for the policyholder. The accumulated assets can be used to create nontaxable permanent insurance or to accumulate tax-deferred capital. Participation is entirely voluntary and all premiums are paid by employees.

guaranteed annual wage (GAW)   A plan that guarantees a minimum annual income to employees.

hardship allowance/premium   An amount of compensation that bears no relation to the work to be done or to living costs, but is paid in recognition of extraordinarily difficult living conditions, harsh environment, isolation, political unrest, or special health problems.

health maintenance organization (HMO)   Prepaid group medical service organization that emphasizes preventive health care. An HMO is defined in the Public Health Service Act (Health Maintenance Organization Act) of 1973 as "an organized system for the delivery of comprehensive health maintenance and treatment services to voluntarily enrolled members for a prenegotiated, fixed periodic payment."

holidays   Specific days when most employees do not work but are paid as if they did. Employees who do work on such days typically receive premium pay or compensatory time off. The number of paid holidays granted by employers varies considerably according to industry group and, to a lesser extent, by geographic region.

hourly   The rate of pay per hour for a job being performed. An "hourly" worker may be assigned to various rated jobs during any pay period and is paid the "rate" applicable to each job while working on it. The term hourly also is used to distinguish between nonexempt and exempt employees, even though so-called hourly or nonexempt employees often are paid on a salaried basis.

incentive compensation   Variable rewards for performance or achievement of short-term or long-term goals. Designed to stimulate employee performance.

incentive stock option (ISO)   A stock option that qualifies for favorable tax treatment (no tax at exercise and long-term capital gains treatment, if shares are held for one year after exercise and two years after grant before sale) and which meets other rules as specified by legislation. The applicable section of the Internal Revenue Code is Section 422.

incentives   Formula-driven pay plans that are designed to reward the accomplishment of specific results. Awards usually are tied to expected results identified at the beginning of the performance cycle. Incentive plans are forward-looking; in contrast to bonuses, they are not discretionary.

indexed options   Options granted which are tied to a specified index of formula and not known on the grant date.

indirect compensation   All forms of nondirect (i.e., noncash) compensation provided to employees in exchange for their contribution to an organization. Indirect compensation most commonly includes benefits. It is called "indirect" because the employer does not pay directly to the employee; for example, it may pay an insurer who provides benefits or a fund that accumulates capital that is used for retirement purposes.

individual pay rate   The wage or salary level assigned to a given individual. Individual pay rates may vary for the same job or as a function of time and grade, performance, or some other basis for establishing variation in the employee's value to the organization.

individual retirement account (IRA)   As specified in the Internal Revenue Code, an individual not covered by an employer-maintained pension plan is eligible to make a tax-deductible contribution to an IRA. A participant covered by an employer-maintained pension may also make a tax-deductible IRA contribution if his/her modified earnings do not exceed the limits specified by law for that year. The $35,000 and $50,000 earnings limits will increase each year beginning in 1999. There will be a sliding scale until 2007. Other participants covered by an employer-provided pension plan may make a nondeductible IRA contribution regardless of their modified earnings. Also, a plan participant receiving a qualifying distribution from a qualified retirement plan may make a "tax-free" rollover directly from the qualified plan to an IRA within a 60-day period.

integrated pension plan   A retirement plan coordinated with Social Security. The plan pays a higher benefit as a percentage of salary for employees in higher salary ranges. The intent is to bring the total benefit (i.e., pension payments plus Social Security payments) as a percentage of salary close to the level of lower-paid employees who receive a greater percentage of salary from Social Security.

intrinsic rewards Rewards that are associated with the job itself, such as the opportunity to perform meaningful work, complete cycles of work, see finished products, experience variety, receive professional development training, enjoy good relations with coworkers and supervisors, and receive feedback on work results. See *extrinsic rewards*.

job The total collection of tasks, duties, and responsibilities assigned to one or more individuals whose work has the same nature and level. Also called a *position*.

job description A summary of the most important features of a job, including the general nature of the work performed (duties and responsibilities) and level (i.e., skill, effort, responsibility, and working conditions) of the work performed. It typically includes job specifications that include employee characteristics required for competent performance of the job. A job description should describe and focus on the job itself and not on any specific individual who might fill the job.

job grade One of the classes, levels, or groups into which jobs of the same or similar value are grouped for compensation purposes. Usually, all jobs in a grade have the same pay range: minimum, midpoint, and maximum. However, sometimes different jobs in the same pay grade have different pay ranges, due to market conditions for some of the jobs.

job satisfaction An indication of how well a person "likes" his or her work, usually determined by a number of factors, including pay, promotional opportunities, supervision, coworkers, and the work itself. When there is a discrepancy between an individual's values and preferences and what the job provides, job satisfaction is reduced.

job sharing An arrangement that allows two or more employees, each working part-time, to share responsibility for a single job and arrange their vacations and days off so that one is always at work during the normal work week.

knowledge, skills, and abilities (KSAs) Common job specifications. Knowledge refers to acquired mental information necessary to do the job (e.g., principles of nuclear physics); skills refer to acquired manual measurable behaviors (e.g., lathe operation); and abilities apply to natural talents or acquired dexterity (e.g., capacity to lift 200 pounds).

knowledge-based pay   A system of salary differentiation based on the formal education, related experience, or specialized training a professional employee has that qualifies the individual to deal with specific subject matter, or to work effectively in a specific field. Salary level may not be dependent on whether the incumbent utilizes the knowledge.

long-term bonus   Usually a form of deferred compensation that establishes an income stream in the form of a bonus over time, typically at a predetermined age or upon retirement.

long-term care insurance   An insurance arrangement that provides care in the event that the insured is unable to perform normal activities of daily living (e.g., bathing, dressing, eating).

long-term disability plan   A form of long-term income protection plan which provides for some continuation of income in the event of disability. Definitions of disability become increasingly narrow in LTD—defining a range of disability, from being disabled from one's own occupation, up to and including being disabled from any occupation at all.

long-term incentive plan   Any incentive plan (usually limited to executives) that requires sustained performance of the firm for a period longer than one fiscal year for maximum benefit to the employee. Some plans are based on capital shares of the organization and may require investment by the employee, while others are based on financial performance.

long-term income protection   Plans that provide financial assistance to workers (1) after they retire, (2) when they incur permanent disabilities that limit or prohibit future employment, (3) to allow them to accumulate capital to provide for their family's future economic well-being, and (4) to protect the family financially in case of death.

major medical insurance   Protection for large surgical, hospital, or other medical expenses and services. Benefits are paid after a specified deductible is met and then generally are subject to coinsurance. Major medical usually is written in conjunction with a basic medical plan and referred to as a *supplementary plan*. If written alone, it is referred to as a *single-plan comprehensive medical program*.

managed care   A plan that attempts to control cost and quality of care by encouraging the utilization of network providers. Examples include health maintenance organizations (HMOs), preferred provider organizations (PPOs), and point-of-service (POS) plans.

mandated benefits   Noncash compensation elements that employers are required by law to provide to their employees (e.g., Social Security, unemployment, workers' compensation).

medical savings (spending) account (MSA)   A medical savings account, or MSA, is a savings account that can be used to pay medical expenses not covered by insurance. Contributions to the plan are deductible from an account holder's federal income tax and, where permitted, from state income tax. Self-employed individuals can accumulate funds in the account from year to year. Self-employed individuals with individual MSAs can make contributions themselves. Employers with small group MSAs may make contributions on behalf of employees, or employees may make the entire contribution.

merit increase   An adjustment to an individual's base pay rate based on performance or some other individual equity basis.

merit progression   A formula for progressing an employee through a wage structure according to performance or some other individual equity basis.

minimum wage   The lowest allowable hourly pay level for most Americans, established by Congress as part of the Fair Labor Standards Act. Some states have laws that mandate higher minimum wages for some employees.

money purchase plan   A type of defined-contribution pension plan in which the employer contribution to the employee's account is based on a formula, regardless of profits.

noncash incentives   Incentive payments that are not readily convertible to cash (e.g., extra time off, meal or merchandise awards, a reserved parking space, or membership in a luncheon club).

noncompete agreements   A provision, or separate employment contract, that prohibits an employee from competing with the employer after termination of employment (or the contract) for a specified period of time.

The agreement typically sets limitations regarding customers, products, services, or an industry (or a combination) after employment terminates.

noncontributory benefit plan   A program in which the employer pays the entire premium or the full cost of funding specific benefits.

nonduplication of benefits   Similar to standard COB, but without allowance for higher benefits between plans. See *coordination of benefits.*

nonexempt employees   A term referring to employees who are not exempt from the minimum wage and overtime pay provisions of the U.S. Fair Labor Standards Act. See *exempt.*

nonqualified pension plan   A plan that provides benefits in excess of those possible within qualified plans, or otherwise does not meet IRS requirements, and therefore does not qualify for favorable tax treatment for the company. See *qualified plan.*

nonqualified stock option (NQSO)   A stock option that does not qualify for special tax treatment under Section 422 of the IRC or which is designated by the company as not being an ISO. Also called a *nonstatutory stock option.* See *stock option.*

on-call pay   A nominal amount of compensation provided in return for an employee being available to report to work at the employer's discretion. Because the employee is expected to be easily reachable and able to report to the work site on short notice, he or she is compensated for having restricted personal time.

out-of-pocket limit   The amount that an employee will pay for covered health-care expenses during the covered period, usually a calendar year, before the plan pays 100 percent of the covered charges.

outplacement assistance   A benefit often made available to employees who are dismissed due to downsizing, reduction in force, or change in business strategy. It typically consists of employment counseling, resume writing, temporary office space, and secretarial assistance.

overtime   Under the Fair Labor Standards Act of 1938 (FLSA), nonexempt employees must be paid one-and-a-half times their normal wage rates for all hours worked in excess of forty in any work week. Some states require overtime be calculated on a basis of other than a forty-hour week.

paid sabbatical   An executive perquisite that provides a paid leave of absence for a specific period of time (e.g., six months) to allow the executive to pursue some outside endeavor (e.g., a civic or charitable project, or completion of an advanced degree).

pay at risk   A variable-pay plan funded on the basis of a reduction in base pay that is usually offset by the possibility of a larger variable-pay plan payout than when base pay is not at risk.

pay for time not worked   Refers to time off work with pay. Typically, it includes the following: holidays, vacations, personal days, jury duty, approved paid leaves, military duty, etc. Also known as *time off with pay.*

pay plan   A schedule of pay rates or ranges for each job in the classification plan. May include rules of administration and the benefit package.

pay range   The range of pay rates, from minimum to maximum, established for a pay grade or class. Typically used to set individual employee pay rates.

pay steps   Specified levels within a pay range. Employees may progress from step to step on the basis of time-in-grade, performance, or the acquisition of new job skills.

pension   A fixed sum of money paid to an employee who has retired from a company and is eligible under a pension plan to receive such benefits. They may be funded (paid from a trust) or unfunded (paid from the company assets).

performance appraisal   Any system of determining how well an individual employee has performed during a period of time, frequently used as a basis for determining merit increases.

performance measurement   Any technique employed to gather data that provides a basis for exercising performance appraisal judgment.

performance share plan (PSP)   A stock (or stock unit) grant award plan contingently granted upon achievement of certain predetermined external or internal performance goals during a specified period (e.g., three to five years) before the recipient has rights to the stock. The employee receiving the shares pays ordinary income tax on the value of the award at the time of earning it. These grants are subject to the variable accounting provisions of APB 25 because the measurement date is the date on which the shares or cash is paid to the participant.

performance sharing (goal sharing)   A process where performance is defined in terms of selected criteria (e.g., quality, customer satisfaction, responsiveness, profit, etc.), standards are established, and incentive awards are made contingent upon meeting these standards, typically at the business-unit or corporate-wide level.

performance unit plan (PUP)   Similar to a performance share plan, except that unit value is not related to stock price. The actual award payment may be in cash, stock, or a combination. See *performance share plan.*

perquisite   A benefit or "perk" tied to a specific key or management-level job (e.g., a company car for personal use, free meals, financial counseling, or use of company facilities). A perk's status value often exceeds its financial value.

person-based pay   Compensation programs that base an employee's salary on that individual's skills or knowledge rather than on the nature of a rigidly defined job. Types include skill-, knowledge-, and competency-based pay.

phantom options   Options or units equivalent to shares but not real shares, or rights to the appreciation on shares without related option rights.

phantom stock   A long-term incentive plan in which the participant receives a payment in cash based on a formula. Under a full-value plan, the full value of the formula is paid. The formula may or may not involve the actual stock price. Incremental-value phantom stock is similar in concept to the full-value phantom stock grant, except that the amount paid is the increase or appreciation in the value as calculated in the formula. The formula may or may not involve the actual stock price.

piece rate   A direct performance payment based on production by an individual worker. A payment made for each piece or other quantity unit of work produced by an employee.

point-of-service (POS)   A type of managed-care medical plan, where the level of benefit received depends on how an employee elects to receive care at the "point of service" where care begins. For example, if care begins with the "gatekeeper" physician in the network, benefits would be higher than if care was received outside the network.

portability   A pension plan feature that allows participants to change employers without changing the source from which benefits are to be paid for both past and future accruals.

preferred provider organization (PPO)   An entity representing a network of health-care providers (e.g., hospitals, physicians, dentists, etc.) that offers volume discounts to employers sponsoring group health benefit plans. In turn, employers commonly extend financial incentives to employees to use participating providers.

premium pay   Extra pay, beyond the base wage rate, for work performed outside or beyond regularly scheduled work periods (e.g., Sundays, holidays, night shifts, etc.). Also may refer to extra pay for high-demand knowledge or skills.

premium stock option   An option whereby the exercise price is set above the fair market value (FMV) at the date of grant.

productivity   Any index measuring the efficiency of an operation, usually involving a ratio of outputs to inputs or costs. Rewards frequently are tied to productivity-related measures.

profit-sharing   A plan providing for employee participation in the profits of an organization. The plan normally includes a predetermined and defined formula for allocating profit shares among participants, and for distributing funds accumulated under the plan. However, some plans are discretionary. Funds may be distributed in cash, deferred as a qualified retirement program, or distributed in a cash/deferred combination.

qualified plan (pension or profit-sharing)   A pension or profit-sharing plan that meets (qualifies under) certain IRS statutory requirements and consequently has certain tax advantages for the employer and/or employee (namely, deferral of employee tax to a future date while still allowing for a current tax deduction for the employer). To qualify, a plan must not discriminate in favor of highly compensated employees. It may be either a defined-benefit or a defined-contribution plan.

rabbi trust   So named because the first such trust approved by the IRS was for a rabbi. A nonqualified trust established by an employer to provide some "psychic" security to employees where the employer promises to pay deferred compensation in the form of cash and/or other assets in the future. The trust is irrevocable and inaccessible to present or future management, and it may or may not be currently funded. It protects against a "change of heart" or a "change of control" in risking nonpayment of promised amounts. However, the funds belong to the corporation, and in the event of bankruptcy, they are specifically within the reach of the organization's creditors.

recognition program   A policy of acknowledging employee contributions after the fact, usually without predetermined goals or performance levels that the employee is expected to achieve. Examples include giving employees clocks or other gifts on milestone anniversaries, granting an extra personal day for perfect attendance, or paying a one-time cash bonus for making a cost-saving suggestion. Also known as *service awards.*

regular rate of pay   Under the Fair Labor Standards Act of 1938 (FLSA), the amount of compensation that is used to calculate overtime rates. The regular rate of pay includes the base rate, shift premium, piece rate, pay allowances, and bonuses.

restricted stock   Stock is given (or sold at a discount) to an employee, who is restricted from selling or transferring it for a specified time period (usually three to five years). The executive receives dividends, but must forfeit the stock if he/she terminates employment before the restriction period ends. If the employee remains in the employ of the company through the restricted period, the shares vest, irrespective of employee or company performance.

rewards system   An organization's choice of cash and noncash motivational elements and the mix of its total compensation program that is used to support its business strategy.

salary   Compensation paid by the week, month, or year (rather than by the hour). Generally applies to jobs that are exempt from the provisions of the Fair Labor Standards Act, but some nonexempt jobs are salaried as well.

salary structure   The hierarchy of job grades and pay ranges established within an organization. The salary structure may be expressed in terms of job grades, job-evaluation points, or policy lines.

sales compensation   Amounts paid to sales representatives or sales management, which vary in accordance with accomplishment of sales goals. Sales compensation formulas usually attempt to establish direct incentives for sales outcomes, such as the establishment of commissions as a percentage of sales.

savings (thrift) plan   A plan established and maintained by an employer to systematically provide for the accumulation of capital by the employees, in accordance with stipulated rates of employee contributions, matched by the employer on the basis of a specified formula.

secular trust   An irrevocable trust established for the exclusive purpose of holding assets to pay employees' nonqualified retirement and/or deferred compensation benefits. It has a design similar to that of a rabbi trust, but the assets contained within the trust are not subject to the claims of the company's general creditors in bankruptcy. It provides benefit payment security to an extent somewhat similar to that provided under a tax-qualified retirement plan trust. The executive is taxed and the company gets a deduction when money is put in the trust. See *rabbi trust.*

seniority   Status determined by the length of time an employee has worked for a given employer, often as the basis for rights, privileges, and benefits. The term also may be used to reflect time worked for a division, group, or specific occupation. Union contracts often provide for multiple seniority calculations.

severance/benefits continuation   Severance is a continuation of an employee's salary after termination that is paid either in a lump sum or on a continuation basis. The amount is generally based on the employee's length of service. Benefits continuation may be a part of a severance package to provide continued coverage under the medical or other benefit plans for the employee and/or dependents for a period after termination.

shift differentials   Extra pay allowances made to employees who work on a shift other than a regular day shift (e.g., 9 a.m. to 5 p.m., Monday through Friday) if the shift is thought to represent a hardship, or if competitive organizations provide a similar premium. Shift differentials usually are expressed as a percentage or in cents per hour.

short-term disability (STD) plan   A benefit plan designed to provide income during absences due to illness or accident, when the employee is expected to return to work within a specified time, usually within six months. Usually coordinated or integrated with sick leave at the beginning and with long-term disability at the end of STD. See *long-term disability plan.*

sick leave   Paid time off provided to employees suffering from illness or nonoccupational injury. Usually coordinated or integrated with short-term disability plans.

simple plan   A type of qualified retirement plan (either IRA or 401[k]) first allowed in 1997, designated for employers with up to 100 employees. No top-heavy or nondiscrimination tests must be passed, but fixed or matching company contributions must be made.

single-rate system   A compensation policy under which all employees in a given job are paid at the same rate instead of being placed in a pay range. Generally applies in situations where there is little room for variation in job performance or skill level.

skill-based pay   A person-based compensation system based on the repertoire of skills an employee can perform rather than the specific skill that the employee may be doing at a particular time. Pay increases generally are associated with the addition and/or improvement of the skills of an individual employee, as opposed to better performance or seniority within the system. Pay level generally is not dependent on whether any of the skills are utilized.

small-group incentive   Any incentive program that focuses on the performance of a small group, usually a work team. These incentive programs are most useful when measurable output is the result of group effort and individual contributions are difficult to separate from the effort of the group.

split-dollar insurance   An agreement between two parties in which each may share in the annual insurance expenses and also may share (according to the terms of the agreement) in the equity and death benefits of the policy. It may be used to secure executive benefits for nonqualified arrangements; this form of split-dollar insurance is known as *corporate-owned life insurance (COLI)*.

stock grant plans   Plans that provide stock to employees without any cost to them. Stock Grants take two basic forms: (1) stock appreciation grants and (2) full-value grants. Stock appreciation grants entitle the employee to the appreciated value of a share of stock (or number of shares or units) over a designated period of time. These grants may be qualified or nonqualified under IRS regulations. A full-value grant entitles the employee to the total value of the worth of the share of stock (or number of shares or units) over a predetermined period of time.

stock option   Rights to purchase company shares at a specified price during a specified period of time.

stock purchase plan   Any program under which employees buy shares in the company's stock. A qualified plan is a program that meets the IRS statutory requirements and results in more favorable benefits and tax treatment for the employee and company. Stock may be offered at a fixed price (usually below market) and paid for in full by employees. A nonqualified plan does not qualify for favorable tax treatment and may include any terms (e.g., discounts below statutory IRS limits).

stock purchase plan (nonqualified)   A plan that is, in effect, a management stock purchase plan. It allows senior management or other key personnel to purchase stock in the business. There are, however, certain restrictions: (1) The stockholder must be employed for a certain period of time. (2) The business has the right to buy back the stock. (3) Stockholders cannot sell the stock for a defined period of time.

stock-appreciation rights (SAR)   An executive-incentive plan in which the corporation grants an executive the right to receive a dollar amount of value equal to the future appreciation of its shares, often in lieu of the executive exercising a share option. An SAR typically is granted as a companion (in tandem) to a share option, and the executive must surrender a matched number of option shares to "cash in" the SAR.

stop-loss provision (health and disability plans)   A provision in a self-funded plan that is designed to limit the risk of employer losses to a specific amount. If claim costs (for a month, a year, or per claim) exceed a predetermined level, an insurance carrier will cover the excess amount. Alternatively, this term may refer to the annual "out-of-pocket maximum" feature in a group medical plan. The out-of-pocket maximum, or employee stop-loss limit, is the most an individual or family must pay in covered expenses, after meeting appropriate deductibles each year.

supplementary executive retirement plan (SERP)   A form of non-qualified pension plan that need not be funded and can be lost if the corporation goes bankrupt. It offers the organization the ability to grant more liberal benefits and to ensure that retirement amounts beyond those authorized under the Employee Retirement Income Security Act of 1974 (ERISA) can be provided to the highly paid employee. SERPs that restore benefits lost under ERISA are called 415 plans because that is the section in the IRS code that describes limits as to qualified plans. Other SERPs are structured to provide benefits (typically for short service) beyond that provided by the basic pension plan.

supplemental unemployment benefits (SUB)   Employer-funded plan that supplements state unemployment insurance payments to workers during temporary periods of layoff. SUB plans are largely concentrated in the automobile, steel, and related industries, and usually are part of a negotiated labor contract.

telecommuting   The process of allowing employees to work at home, most likely with the availability of computer and fax links to the office.

term insurance   A renewable life insurance contract that specifies beginning and ending dates for coverage and which has no cash value at termination.

total annual cash compensation   The sum of all cash payments made to an individual for services (i.e., employment) during a given year. See *total compensation.*

total compensation   The complete reward/recognition package for employees, including all forms of money, benefits, perquisites, services, and in-kind payments.

total remuneration   The sum of the financial and nonfinancial value to the employee of all the elements in the employment package (i.e., salary, incentives, benefits, perquisites, job satisfaction, organizational affiliation, status, etc.) and any other intrinsic or extrinsic rewards of the employment exchange that the employee values.

unemployment insurance State-administered programs that provide financial protection for workers during periods of joblessness. These plans are wholly financed by employers except in Alabama, Alaska, New Jersey, and Pennsylvania, where there are provisions for relatively small employee contributions. Also known as *unemployment compensation* or *unemployment benefits.*

variable pay Rewards based on individual, group, or organizational performance rather than rewards based on time spent on the job or the value of the job.

vesting (1) Typically used in conjunction with a pension plan or a stock plan. Under a pension plan it assures that a participant will, after meeting certain requirements, retain a right to the benefits he or she has accrued (or some portion of them), even if employment under the plan terminates before retirement. Employee contributions are always fully vested. (2) For a stock option, it is the time when an executive's stock option or stock appreciation right becomes exercisable, or when other executive compensation becomes nonforfeitable.

wage differential Differences in wage rates (for similar jobs) that can occur because of location of company, hours of work, working conditions, type of product manufactured, or a variety of other circumstances.

wage rate The money rate, expressed in dollars and cents, paid to an employee per hour.

welfare plan Plans that provide dental, vision, disability, life insurance, medical, surgical, or hospital care, or benefits in the case of sickness, accident, death, or unemployment. Under the Employee Retirement Income Security Act of 1974 (ERISA), they also may include other benefits, such as vacation or scholarship plans.

workers' compensation insurance State laws that have the goals of providing: (1) medical care or cash payment to cover health services for workers injured on the job or due to a job-related illness, (2) partial wage-replacement benefits, and (3) rehabilitation services to restore workers to their fullest economic capacity. All benefits are totally employer-financed.

Index

More Good Books from JIST Works, Inc.

Résumé Magic
By Susan Britton Whitcomb

At last—a professional résumé writer reveals her inside trade secrets for creating phenomenal résumés. Now, you too can create fabulous résumés by following her advice.

No other book explains the nuts and bolts of résumé writing so clearly. The author takes you step-by-step through the process of crafting a résumé as a marketing piece, providing a quick course in "résumé speak," a unique style of writing that combines advertising and business formats to give your résumé energy and interest.

8⅜ × 10⅞, paper, 596 pp.
ISBN 1-56370-522-2 • $18.95 (higher in Canada)

Healthy, Wealthy, & Wise:
A Guide to Retirement Planning
Compiled by the editors at Drake Beam Morin

This easy-to-follow strategy guide makes retirement planning easy—and effective.

Whether you want to relax in a rocking chair or fill your days with new adventures, *Healthy, Wealthy, & Wise* shows you how to make your retirement the best time of your life!

Exercises, worksheets, and expert tips lead you step-by-step to the retirement lifestyle of your dreams.

6 × 9, paper, 208 pp.
ISBN 1-57112-081-5 • $12.95 (higher in Canada)

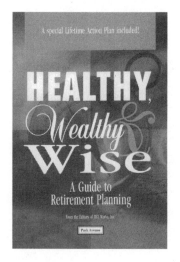

Look for these and other fine books from JIST Works at your full-service bookstore, or call us at 1-800-648-JIST